C-671

ISBN 0-8373-0671-X

THE PASSBOOK® SERIES

PASSBOOKS®

FOR

CAREER OPPORTUNITIES

REGISTERED PROFESSIONAL NURSE

National Learning Corporation

212 Michael Drive, Syosset, New York 11791

(516) 921-8888

National Learning Corporation
212 Michael Drive, Syosset, New York 11791
(516) 921-8888

PRINTED IN THE UNITED STATES OF AMERICA

PASSBOOK®

NOTICE

This book is *SOLELY* intended for, is sold *ONLY* to, and its use is *RESTRICTED* to *individual*, bona fide applicants or candidates who qualify by virtue of having seriously filed applications for appropriate license, certificate, professional and/or promotional advancement, higher school matriculation, scholarship, or other legitimate requirements of educational and/or governmental authorities.

This book is *NOT* intended for use, class instruction, tutoring, training, duplication, copying, reprinting, excerption, or adaptation, etc., by:

(1) Other Publishers
(2) Proprietors and/or Instructors of "Coaching" and/or Preparatory Courses
(3) Personnel and/or Training Divisions of commercial, industrial, and governmental organizations
(4) Schools, colleges, or universities and/or their departments and staffs, including teachers and other personnel
(5) Testing Agencies or Bureaus
(6) Study groups which seek by the purchase of a single volume to copy and/or duplicate and/or adapt this material for use by the group as a whole without having purchased individual volumes for each of the members of the group
(7) Et al.

Such persons would be in violation of appropriate Federal and State statutes.

PROVISION OF LICENSING AGREEMENTS. — Recognized educational commercial, industrial, and governmental institutions and organizations, and others legitimately engaged in educational pursuits, including training, testing, and measurement activities, may address a request for a licensing agreement to the copyright owners, who will determine whether, and under what conditions, including fees and charges, the materials in this book may be used by them. In other words, a licensing facility *exists* for the legitimate use of the material in this book on other than an individual basis. However, it is asseverated and affirmed here that the materials in this book *CANNOT* be used without the receipt of the express permission of such a licensing agreement from the Publishers.

NATIONAL LEARNING CORPORATION
212 Michael Drive
Syosset, New York 11791

Inquiries re licensing agreements should be addressed to:
The President
National Learning Corporation
212 Michael Drive
Syosset, New York 11791

PASSBOOK SERIES®

THE PASSBOOK SERIES® has been created to prepare applicants and candidates for the ultimate academic battlefield—the examination room.

AT SOME time in our lives, each and every one of us may be required to take an examination—for validation, matriculation, admission, qualification, registration, certification, or licensure.

BASED ON the assumption that every applicant or candidate has met the basic formal educational standards, has taken the required number of courses, and read the necessary texts, the PASSBOOK SERIES® furnishes the one special preparation which may assure passing with confidence, instead of failing with insecurity. Examination questions—together with answers—are furnished as the basic vehicle for study so that the mysteries of the examination and its compounding difficulties may be eliminated or diminished by a sure method.

THIS BOOK is meant to help you pass your examination provided that you qualify and are serious in your objective.

THE ENTIRE field is reviewed through the huge store of content information which is succinctly presented through a provocative and challenging approach—the question-and-answer method.

A CLIMATE of success is established by furnishing the correct answers at the end of each test.

YOU SOON learn to recognize types of questions, forms of questions, and patterns of questioning. You may even begin to anticipate expected outcomes.

YOU PERCEIVE that many questions are repeated or adapted so that you gain acute insights, which may enable you to score many sure points.

YOU LEARN how to confront new questions, or types of questions, and to attack them confidently and work out the correct answers.

YOU NOTE objectives and emphases, and recognize pitfalls and dangers, so that you may make positive educational adjustments.

MOREOVER, you are kept fully informed in relation to new concepts, methods, practices, and directions in the field.

YOU DISCOVER that you are actually taking the examination all the time: you are preparing for the examination by "taking" an examination, not by reading extraneous and/or supererogatory textbooks.

IN SHORT, this PASSBOOK®, used directedly, should be an important factor in helping you to pass your test.

REGISTERED NURSES

NATURE OF THE WORK

Nursing care plays a major role in providing health care. As important members of the medical care team, registered nurses perform a wide variety of duties. They administer medications; observe, evaluate, and record symptoms, reactions, and progress of patients; assist in the rehabilitation of patients; and help maintain a physical and emotional environment that promotes patient recovery.

Some registered nurses provide hospital care. Others perform research activities or instruct students. The type of employment setting usually determines the scope of the nurse's duties.

Hospital nurses constitute the largest group. Most are staff nurses who provide skilled bedside nursing care and carry out medical treatment plans prescribed by physicians. They may also supervise practical nurses, aides, and orderlies. Hospital nurses usually work with groups of patients that require similar nursing care. For instance, some nurses work with post-surgery patients; others care for children, the elderly, or the mentally ill. Some are administrators of nursing services.

Private duty nurses give individual care to patients who need constant attention. The private duty nurse may sometimes care for several hospital patients who require special care, but not full-time attention.

Office nurses assist physicians, dental surgeons, and occasionally dentists in private practice or clinics. Sometimes they perform routine laboratory and office work in addition to their nursing duties.

Public Health nurses care for patients in clinics, homes, schools and other community settings. They instruct patients and families in proper care, and give periodic care as prescribed by a physician. They may also instruct groups of patients in proper diet and arrange for immunizations. These nurses work with community leaders, teachers, parents, and physicians in community health education. Smme public health nurses work in schools.

Nurse educators teach students the principles and skills of nursing, both in the classroom and in direct patient care. They also conduct continuing education courses for registered nurses, practical nurses and nursing assistants.

Occupational health or industrial nurses provide nursing care to employees in industry and government, and along with physicians promote employee health. As prescribed by a doctor, they treat minor injuries and illnesses occurring at the place of employment, provide for the needed nursing care, arrange for further medical care if necessary, and offer health counseling.

They also may assist with health examinations and inoculations.

(Licensed practical nurses who also perform nursing service are discussed elsewhere.)

PLACES OF EMPLOYMENT

Nearly 750,000 persons - all but 1 percent women - worked as registered nurses. About one-third of them worked on a part-time basis.

More than two-thirds of all registered nurses worked in hospitals, nursing homes, and related institutions. About 60,000 were office nurses and about 50,000 were private duty nurses who cared for patients in hospitals and private homes. Public health nurses in government agencies, schools, visiting nurse associations, and clinics numbered about 54,000; nurse educators in nursing schools accounted for about 35,000; and occupational health nurses in industry, about 20,000. Most of the others were staff members of professional nurse and other organizations, State boards of nursing, or working for research organizations.

TRAINING, OTHER QUALIFICATIONS, AND ADVANCEMENT

A license is required to practice professional nursing in all States and in the District of Columbia. To obtain a license, a nurse must be a graduate of a school approved by the State board of nursing and pass the State board examination. Nurses may be licensed in more than one State, either by examination or endorsement of a license issued by another State.

Three types of educational programs - diploma, baccalaureate, and associate degree - offer the education required for basic careers in registered nursing. Education at the master's level and above is required for positions in research, consultation, teaching, and clinical specialization. Graduation from high school is required for admission to all schools of nursing.

Diploma programs are conducted by hospital and independent schools and usually require 3 years of training. Bachelor's degree programs usually require 4 years of study in a college or university, although a few require 5 years. Associate degree programs in junior and community colleges require approximately 2 years of nursing education. In addition, several programs provide licensed practical nurses with the training necessary to upgrade themselves to registered nurses while they continue to work part-time. These programs generally offer an associate of arts degree. More than 1,360 programs (associate, diploma, and baccalaureate) were offered in the United States. In addition, about 80 colleges and universities offered master's and doctoral degree programs in nursing.

Programs of nursing include classroom instruction and supervised nursing practice in hospitals and health facilities. Students take courses in anatomy, physiology, microbiology, nutrition, psychology, and basic nursing care. They also get supervised clinical experience in the care of patients who have different types of health problems. Students in bachelor's degree programs as well as in some of the other programs are assigned to public health agencies to learn how to care for patients in clinics and in the patients' homes. General education is combined with nursing education in baccalaureate and associate degree programs and in some diploma programs.

Qualified students who need financial aid can get a nursing scholarship or a low-interest loan under the provisions of the Nurse Training Act of 1971.

Depending on length of service, up to 85 percent of the loan can be cancelled over a 5-year period for full-time employment as a professional nurse in any public or nonprofit institution or agency. Full-time employment in an area identified as a shortage area can make one eligible for cancellation of 85 percent of the loan over a three-year period.

Young persons who want to pursue a nursing career should have a sincere desire to serve humanity and be sympathetic to the needs of others. Nurses must be able to follow orders precisely and to use good judgment in emergencies; they also should be able to accept responsibility and direct or supervise the activity of others. Good mental health is helpful in order to cope with human suffering and frequent emergency situations. Staff nurses may need physical stamina because of the amount of time spent walking and standing.

From staff positions in hospitals, experienced nurses may advance to head nurse, assistant director, and director of nursing services. A master's degree, however, often is required for supervisory and administrative positions, as well as for positions in nursing education, clinical specialization, and research. In public health agencies, advancement is usually difficult for nurses who do not have degrees in public health nursing.

A growing movement in nursing, generally being referred to as the "nurse practitioner program", is opening up new career possibilities. Nurses who wish to take the extra training are preparing for highly independent roles in the clinical care and teaching of patients. They are practicing in primary roles which include nurse-midwifery, maternal care, pediatrics, family health, and the care of medical patients.

EMPLOYMENT OUTLOOK

Employment opportunities for registered nurses are expected to be favorable through the mid-1990's. However, if trends in the number of persons enrolling in schools of nursing continue, some competition for more desirable, higher paying jobs may develop by the mid-1990's. Opportunities for full- or part-time work in present shortage areas such as some Southern States and many innercity areas are expected to be very favorable through 1995. For nurses who have had graduate education, the outlook is excellent for obtaining positions as administrators, teachers, clinical specialists, public health nurses, and for work in research.

A very rapid increase in employment of registered nurses is expected because of rising population, improved economic status of the population, extension of prepayment programs for hospitalization and medical care, expansion of medical services as a result of new medical techniques and drugs, and increased interest in preventive medicine and rehabilitation of the handicapped. In addition to the need to fill new positions, large numbers of nurses will be required to replace those who leave the field each year because of marriage and family responsibilities.

EARNINGS AND WORKING CONDITIONS

Registered nurses in nursing homes can expect to earn slightly less than those in hospitals.

Most hospital nurses receive extra pay for work on evening or night shifts. Nearly all receive at least 2 weeks of paid vacation after 1 year of service. Most hospital nurses receive from 5 to 13 paid holidays a year and also some type of health and retirement benefits.

SOURCES OF ADDITIONAL INFORMATION

For information on approved schools of nursing, nursing careers, loans, scholarships, salaries, working conditions, and employment opportunities, contact:

> ANA Committee on Nursing Careers, American Nurses' Association, 2420 Pershing Road, Kansas City, MO. 64108.

Information about employment opportunities in the Veterans Administration is available from:

> Department of Medicine and Surgery, Veterans Administration, Washington, D.C. 20420

How to Take a Test

You have studied hard, long, and conscientiously.

With your official admission card in hand, and your heart pounding, you have been admitted to the examination room.

You note that there are several hundred other applicants in the examination room waiting to take the same test.

They all appear to be equally well prepared.

You know that nothing but your best effort will suffice. The "moment of truth" is at hand: you now have to demonstrate objectively, in writing, your knowledge of content and your understanding of subject matter.

You are fighting the most important battle of your life—to pass and/or score high on an examination which will determine your career and provide the economic basis for your livelihood.

What extra, special things should you know and should you do in taking the examination?

Before the Test

Your Physical Condition Is Important

If you are not well, you can't do your best work on tests. If you are half asleep, you can't do your best either. Here are some tips:

1. Get about the same amount of sleep you usually get. Don't stay up all night before the test, either partying or worrying—DON'T DO IT.
2. If you wear glasses, be sure to wear them when you go to take the test. This goes for hearing aids, too.
3. If you have any physical problems that may keep you from doing your best, be sure to tell the person giving the test. If you are sick or in poor health, you really cannot do your best on any test. You can always come back and take the test some other time.

At the Test

Examination Techniques

1. Read the *general* instructions carefully. These are usually printed on the first page of the examination booklet. As a rule, these instructions refer to the timing of the examination; the fact that you should not start work until the signal and must stop work at a signal, etc. If there are any *special* instructions, such as a choice of questions to be answered, make sure that you note this instruction carefully.

2. When you are ready to start work on the examination, that is as soon as the signal has been given, read the instructions to each question booklet, underline any key words or phrases, such as *least, best, outline, describe*, and the like. In this way you will tend to answer as requested rather than discover on reviewing your paper that you *listed without describing,* that you selected the *worst* choice rather than the *best* choice, etc.

3. If the examination is of the objective or so-called multiple-choice type, that is, each question will also give a series of possible answers: A, B, C, or D, and you are called upon to select the best answer and write the letter next to that answer on your answer paper, it is advisable to start answering each question in turn. There may be anywhere from 50 to 100 such questions in the three or four hours allotted and you can see how much time would be taken if you read through all the questions before beginning to answer any. Furthermore, if you come across a question or a group of questions which you know would be difficult to answer, it would undoubtedly affect your handling of all the other questions.

4. If the examination is of the essay-type and contains but a few questions, it is a moot point as to whether you should read all the questions before starting to answer any one. Of course if you are given a choice, say five out of seven and the like, then it is essential to read all the questions so you can eliminate the two which are most difficult. If, however, you are asked to answer all the questions, there may be danger in trying to answer the easiest one first because you may find that you will spend too much time on it. The best technique is to answer the first question, then proceed to the second, etc.

5. Time your answers. Before the examination begins, write down the time it started, then add the time allowed for the examination and write down the time it must be completed, then divide the time available somewhat as follows:
   - **a.** If 3 ½ hours are allowed, that would be 210 minutes. If you have 80 objective-type questions, that would be an average of about 2 ½ minutes per question. Allow yourself no more than 2 minutes per question, or a total of 160 minutes, which will permit about 50 minutes to review.
   - **b.** If for the time allotment of 210 minutes, there are 7 essay questions to answer, that would average about 30 minutes a question. Give yourself only 25 minutes per question so that you have about 35 minutes to review.

6. The most important instruction is *to read each question* and make sure you know what is wanted. The second most important instruction is to *time yourself properly* so that you answer every question. The third most important instruction is to *answer every question*. Guess if you have to but include something for each question, Remember that you will receive no credit for a blank and will probably receive some credit if you write something in answer to an essay question. If you guess a letter, say "B" for a multiple-choice question, you may have guessed right. If you leave a blank as the answer to a multiple-choice question, the examiners may respect your feelings but it will not add a point to your score. Some exams may penalize you for wrong answers, so in such cases *only*, you may not want to guess unless you have some basis for your answer.

7. Suggestions

   a. Objective-Type Questions

      (1) Examine the question booklet for proper sequence of pages and questions.
      (2) Read all instructions carefully.
      (3) Skip any question which seems too difficult; return to it after all other questions have been answered.
      (4) Apportion your time properly; do not spend too much time on any single question or group of questions.
      (5) Note and underline key words—*all, most, fewest, least, best, worst, same, opposite.*
      (6) Pay particular attention to negatives.
      (7) Note unusual option, e.g., unduly long, short, complex, different or similar in content to the body of the question.
      (8) Observe the use of "hedging" words—*probably, may, most likely, etc.*
      (9) Make sure that your answer is put next to the same number as the question.
      (10) Do not second guess unless you have good reason to believe the second answer is definitely more correct.
      (11) Cross out original answer if you decide another answer is more accurate; do not erase, *until* you are ready to hand your paper in.
      (12) Answer all questions; guess unless instructed otherwise.
      (13) Leave time for review.

b. Essay-Type Questions

(1) Read each question carefully.

(2) Determine exactly what is wanted. Underline key words or phrases.

(3) Decide on outline or paragraph answer.

(4) Include many different points and elements unless asked to develop any one or two points or elements.

(5) Show impartiality by giving pros and cons unless directed to select one side only.

(6) Make and write down any assumptions you find necessary to answer the question.

(7) Watch your English, grammar, punctuation, choice of words.

(8) Time your answers; don't crowd material.

8. Answering the Essay Question

Most essay questions can be answered by framing the specific response around several key words or ideas. Here are a few such key words or ideas:

M's: manpower, materials, methods, money, management

P's: purpose, program, policy, plan, procedure, practice, problems, pitfalls, personnel, public relations

a. Six basic steps in handling problems:

(1) preliminary plan and background development

(2) collect information, data and facts

(3) analyze and interpret information, data and facts

(4) analyze and develop solutions as well as make recommendations

(5) prepare report and sell recommendations

(6) install recommendations and follow up effectiveness

b. Pitfalls to Avoid

(1) *Taking Things for Granted*
A statement of the situation does not necessarily imply that each of the elements is necessarily true; for example, a complaint may be invalid and biased so that all that can be taken for granted is that a complaint has been registered

(2) *Considering only one side of a situation*
Wherever possible, indicate several alternatives and then point out the reasons you selected the best one.

(3) *Failing to indicate follow up*
Whenever your answer indicates action on your part, make certain that you will take proper follow-up action to see how successful your recommendations, procedures, or actions turn out to be.

(4) *Taking too long in answering any single question*
Remember to time your answers properly.

EXAMINATION SECTION

EXAMINATION SECTION

TEST 1

DIRECTIONS: Each question or incomplete statement is followed by several suggested answers or completions. Select the one that BEST answers the question or completes the statement. *PRINT THE LETTER OF THE CORRECT ANSWER IN THE SPACE AT THE RIGHT.*

Questions 1-10.

DIRECTIONS: Questions 1 through 10 are to be answered on the basis of the following information.

Ms. Martha McCarthy, 32 years old, is brought to the emergency unit on a stretcher. Ms. McCarthy was in an automobile accident and is conscious upon admission. X-rays show that she has considerable vertebral damage at the level of T-6. The surgical unit is notified that Ms. McCarthy will be brought directly from the x-ray department.

1. Which of the facts about Ms. McCarthy, if obtained when she is admitted to the hospital, would MOST likely require early intervention? 1.___
She
   A. is a vegetarian
   B. last voided 7 hours ago
   C. smokes 2 packs of cigarettes a day
   D. is menstruating

2. Twelve hours after admission, Ms. McCarthy begins to develop some difficulty in breathing. 2.___
In addition to obtaining a respirator and calling the physician, the nurse would show the BEST judgment by
   A. turning Ms. McCarthy onto her abdomen to promote drainage from the mouth and throat
   B. encouraging Ms. McCarthy to exercise her upper extremities at intervals
   C. elevating the foot of Ms. McCarthy's bed
   D. bringing pharyngeal suction equipment to Ms. McCarthy's bedside

3. Considering the level of Ms. McCarthy's injury (T-6), it is MOST justifiable to assume that her respiratory difficulty is due to 3.___
   A. edema of the cord above the level of injury
   B. hemorrhage into the brain stem due to trauma
   C. movement of the parts of the fractured vertebrae
   D. severing of the nerves that activate the diaphragm

4. The nurse can prevent Ms. McCarthy's lower extremities from rotating externally by placing 4.___
   A. her feet against a footboard
   B. pillows against her calves
   C. trochanter rolls along the inner aspects of her knees
   D. sandbags against the outer aspects of her thighs

5. Ms. McCarthy is to have a laminectomy. 5.___
The CHIEF purpose of a laminectomy for her is to
   A. realign the vertebral fragments
   B. relieve pressure on the cord
   C. repair spinal nerve damage
   D. reduce spinal fluid pressure

6. Ms. McCarthy is highly susceptible to the development of decubitus ulcers because 6.___
   A. an intact nervous system is necessary for maintenance of normal tone of blood vessels
   B. flexor muscles have a greater loss of tone than extensor muscles
   C. decreased permeability of the capillary walls results from central nervous system damage
   D. atonic muscles have an increased need for oxygen

7. Ms. McCarthy has a laminectomy and spinal fusion. The physician tells her that she will not be able to walk without the use of supportive devices. 7.___
Before surgery, Ms. McCarthy should have been informed that the bone to be used as a graft for a spinal fusion is MOST likely to be obtained from the
   A. posterior iliac crest
   B. adjacent sacral vertebrae
   C. humerus
   D. sternum

8. The nursing staff notices a pronounced change in Ms. McCarthy's behavior after the physician discusses her prognosis with her. She is now overtly rebellious, responding negatively to personnel, to treatments, and to nursing measures. 8.___
The interpretation of her behavior is that she is
   A. unable to face the prospect of a long rehabilitative program
   B. projecting her own unhappiness onto others
   C. reacting to the change in her body image
   D. seeking punishment for feelings of guilt about her injury

9. A rehabilitative program is started for Ms. McCarthy. She is to wear leg braces. 9.___
When applying Ms. McCarthy's leg braces, it is ESSENTIAL for the nurse to consider that Ms. McCarthy
   A. cannot move her lower extremities
   B. has no sensation in her lower extremities
   C. can flex her knees to a 45-degree angle
   D. cannot fully extend her hip joints

10. To achieve success in a rehabilitation program for Ms. McCarthy, the MOST important information about Ms. McCarthy is her 10.___
   A. knowledge of services available to her
   B. personal goals
   C. being encouraged by her family
   D. relationship with members of the health team

Questions 11-16.

DIRECTIONS: Questions 11 through 16 are to be answered on the basis of the following information.

Ms. Beth Marks, a 21-year-old college student, sustains a head injury as a result of a fall down a flight of stairs. She is brought to the emergency room with a pronounced swelling of the forehead. She is admitted to the hospital for observation.

11. On admission, Ms. Marks' blood pressure was 110/80, her pulse rate was 88, and her respiratory rate was 20. It would be MOST indicative of increasing intracranial pressure if her blood pressure, pulse, and respirations were, respectively, 11.___
   A. 90/54; 50; 22
   B. 100/66; 120; 32
   C. 120/90; 96; 16
   D. 140/70; 60; 14

12. Ms. Marks' condition worsens. She has a craniotomy, and a hematoma is removed. Her postoperative orders include elevation of the head of her bed, and mannitol. When Ms. Marks reacts from anesthesia, she is put in a semi-reclining position to 12.___
   A. increase thoracic expansion and facilitate oxygenation of damaged tissue
   B. provide adequate drainage and prevent fluid accumulation in the cranial cavity
   C. decrease cardiac workload and prevent hemorrhage at the surgical site
   D. reduce pressure in the subarachnoid space and promote tissue granulation

13. It is CORRECT to say that in this case mannitol is expected to 13.___
   A. decrease body fluids
   B. elevate the filtration rate in the kidney
   C. control filtration of nitrogenous wastes
   D. increase the volume of urine

14. The PRIMARY purpose of administering mannitol to Ms. Marks is to 14.___
   A. promote kidney function
   B. prevent bladder distention
   C. reduce cerebral pressure
   D. diminish peripheral fluid retention

15. Eight hours after surgery, Ms. Marks' temperature rises to 104°F. (40°C.), and a hypothermia blanket is ordered for her. 15.___
Ms. Marks' temperature elevation is MOST likely due to a(n)
   A. accumulation of respiratory secretions resulting from inadequate ventilation
   B. alteration of metabolism resulting from pressure on the hypothalamus
   C. increase in leukocytosis resulting from bacterial invasion
   D. constriction of the main artery in the circle of Willis resulting from a ventricular fluid shift

16. Following a craniotomy, a patient may be given caffeine and sodium benzoate to 16.___
   A. lessen cerebral irritation by depressing the cerebrum
   B. improve the sense of touch by blocking spinal nerve reflexes
   C. enable commands to be followed by activating the medullary cells
   D. increase mental alertness by stimulating the cerebral cortex

Questions 17-25.

DIRECTIONS: Questions 17 through 25 are to be answered on the basis of the following information.

Mr. Paul Peters, 61 years old, is admitted to the hospital. Vascular occlusion of his left leg is suspected, and he is scheduled for an arteriogram.

17. The nurse is to assess the circulation in Mr. Peters' lower extremities. 17.___
Which of these measures would be ESPECIALLY significant?
   A. Comparing the pulses in the lower extremities
   B. Comparing the temperatures of the lower extremities
   C. Noting the pulse in the left leg
   D. Noting the temperature of the left leg

18. Which of these symptoms manifested in Mr. Peters' affected left extremity would indicate that he has intermittent claudication? 18.___
   A. Extensive discoloration
   B. Dependent edema
   C. Pain associated with activity
   D. Petechiae

19. Following Mr. Peters' admission, an IMMEDIATE goal in his care should be to 19.___
   A. improve the muscular strength of his extremities
   B. achieve maximum rehabilitation for him
   C. prevent the extension of his disease process
   D. protect his extremities from injury

20. During the night following his admission, Mr. Peters says that he can't sleep because his feet are cold. 20.___
The nurse should
A. offer Mr. Peters a warm drink
B. massage Mr. Peters' feet briskly for several minutes
C. ask Mr. Peters if he has any socks with him
D. place a heating pad under Mr. Peters' feet

21. Information given to Mr. Peters about the femoral arteriogram should include the fact that 21.___
A. a local anesthetic will be given to lessen discomfort
B. there are minimal risks associated with the procedure
C. the radioactive dye that is injected will be removed before he returns to his unit
D. a radiopaque substance will be injected directly into the small vessels of his feet

22. When Mr. Peters is brought back to his unit following the arteriogram, which of these actions would be appropriate? 22.___
A. Encourage fluid intake and have him lie prone
B. Apply heat to the site used for introducing the intravenous catheter and passively exercise his involved extremity
C. Limit motion of his affected extremity and check the site used for the injection of the dye
D. Restrict his fluid intake and encourage him to ambulate

23. The results of Mr. Peters' arteriogram revealed a marked narrowing of the left femoral artery. He has a venous graft bypass performed. Following a stay in the recovery room, he is returned to his room. 23.___
The postoperative care plan for Mr. Peters should include which of these notations?
A. Keep the affected extremity elevated
B. Check the pulse distal to the graft site
C. Check for color changes proximal to the proximal site
D. Check for fine movements of the toes

24. During the first postoperative day, Mr. Peters is kept on bed rest. 24.___
Which of these exercises for Mr. Peters would it be APPROPRIATE for the nurse to initiate?
A. Straight leg raising of both lower extremities
B. Range of motion of both lower extremities
C. Abduction of the affected extremity
D. Dorsiflexion and extension of the foot of the affected extremity

25. When Mr. Peters returns to bed after ambulating, it would be MOST important for the nurse to check 25.___
A. his blood pressure
B. his radial pulse
C. the temperature of his affected extremity
D. the pedal pulse of his affected extremity

KEY (CORRECT ANSWERS)

1. B
2. D
3. A
4. D
5. B

6. A
7. A
8. C
9. B
10. B

11. D
12. B
13. D
14. C
15. B

16. D
17. A
18. C
19. D
20. C

21. A
22. C
23. B
24. D
25. D

TEST 2

DIRECTIONS: Each question or incomplete statement is followed by several suggested answers or completions. Select the one that BEST answers the question or completes the statement. *PRINT THE LETTER OF THE CORRECT ANSWER IN THE SPACE AT THE RIGHT.*

Questions 1-8.

DIRECTIONS: Questions 1 through 8 are to be answered on the basis of the following information.

Three days ago, Susan Cooper, 4 years old, was admitted to the hospital with a diagnosis of heart failure. She was digitalized the day of her admission and is now to receive a maintenance dose of digoxin (Lanoxin) 0.08 mg. p.o.b.i.d. Susan has been under medical supervision for cystic fibrosis and has severe pulmonary involvement.

1. The stock bottle of Lanoxin contains 0.05 mg. of the drug in 1 cc. of solution. How much solution will contain a single dose (0.08 mg.) of the drug for Susan? 1.___
_____ cc.
A. 0.06 B. 0.6 C. 1.6 D. 2.6

2. Prior to the administration of a dose of Lanoxin to Susan, the nurse should take her _____ pulse. 2.___
A. femoral
B. apical
C. radial
D. both apical and radial

3. The nurse would be CORRECT in withholding Susan's dose of Lanoxin without specific instructions from the doctor if Susan's pulse rate were below _____ beats per minute. 3.___
A. 100 B. 115 C. 130 D. 145

4. Which of these measures is likely to be MOST helpful in providing for Susan's nutritional needs while she is acutely ill? 4.___
A. Serving her food lukewarm
B. Giving her only liquids that she can take through a straw
C. Offering her small portions of favorite foods frequently
D. Mixing her foods together so that they are not readily identifiable

5. Because Susan has symptoms of acute cardiac failure, her oral feedings will DIFFER from the feedings of a normal child the same age in the 5.___
A. size of the feedings *only*
B. rapidity and size of the feedings
C. frequency and rapidity of the feedings
D. size, rapidity, and frequency of the feedings

6. All of the following information is part of Susan's health history. 6.___
Which fact relates MOST directly to a diagnosis of cystic fibrosis?
   A. Emergency surgery as a newborn for intestinal obstruction
   B. Jaundice that lasted 4 days during the newborn period
   C. A temperature of 104°F. (40°C.) followed by a convulsion when she was 6 months old
   D. A left otitis media treated with antibiotics when she was 12 months old

7. Susan is placed in a mist tent in order to 7.___
   A. increase the hydration of secretions
   B. prevent the loss of fluids through evaporation
   C. aid in maintaining a therapeutic environmental temperature
   D. improve the transport of oxygen and carbon dioxide

8. Susan is receiving pancreatin replacement therapy to promote the absorption of 8.___
   A. protein
   B. carbohydrate
   C. vitamin C (ascorbic acid)
   D. sodium

Questions 9-13.

DIRECTIONS: Questions 9 through 13 are to be answered on the basis of the following information.

Ms. Leslie Browne, a 21-year-old college student, is seen by a physician because of fatigue and weight loss. Physical examination reveals slight enlargement of her cervical lymph nodes. Ms. Browne is admitted to the hospital for diagnostic studies.

9. Ms. Browne states that she has had a low-grade fever. 9.___
Which of these questions pertaining to Ms. Browne's low-grade fever should the nurse ask INITIALLY?
   A. When did you first notice that your temperature had gone up?
   B. Has your temperature been over 102 degrees?
   C. Have you recently been exposed to anyone who has an infection?
   D. Do you have a sore throat?

10. Ms. Browne is to have a chest x-ray and is to be transported to the x-ray department by stretcher. 10.___
All of the following actions may be taken by the nurse when sending Ms. Browne for the x-ray.
Which action is ESSENTIAL?
   A. Strap Ms. Browne securely to the stretcher.
   B. Place Ms. Browne's chart under the mattress of the stretcher.
   C. Ask Ms. Browne to remove her wristwatch.
   D. Assign a nurse's aide to accompany Ms. Browne.

11. The results of diagnostic tests establish that Ms. Browne has Hodgkin's disease with involvement of the cervical and mediastinal nodes. She is to have an initial course of intravenous chemotherapy with mechlorethamine (Mustargen) hydrochloride. The Mustargen that Ms. Browne receives is administered to her through the tubing of a rapidly flowing intravenous infusion. 11.___
The purpose of this method of administration is to
   A. reduce the half-life of the medication
   B. minimize the side effects of the medication
   C. decrease irritation of the blood vessel by the medication
   D. control the rate of absorption of the medication

12. While Ms. Browne is receiving Mustargen therapy, she is MOST likely to develop 12.___
   A. alopecia
   B. fecal impactions
   C. temporary neuropathy
   D. transient nausea

13. The insertion site of Ms. Browne's intravenous infusion is edematous. 13.___
Which of these actions should the nurse take?
   A. Lower the height of the infusion container
   B. Discontinue the infusion
   C. Flush the infusion tubing with 5 ml. of isotonic saline solution
   D. Reduce the rate of infusion

Questions 14-25.

DIRECTIONS: Questions 14 through 25 are to be answered on the basis of the following information.

Mr. Robert Dine, a 66-year-old widower who has diabetes mellitus, is admitted to the hospital in metabolic acidosis. He has gangrene of the great toe of his left foot and ulceration of the heel.

14. Immediately after Mr. Dine's admission, the nurse places him on his side and then at frequent intervals turns him from side to side. 14.___
The CHIEF purpose of these actions is to
   A. reduce the possibility of pulmonary embolism
   B. insure maximal circulation in the gangrenous extremity
   C. promote the exchange of oxygen and carbon dioxide
   D. facilitate the breakdown of lactic acid

15. Because Mr. Dine has a gangrenous toe and a heel ulcer, which of the following equipment is ESSENTIAL to his care? 15.___
   A. Sheepskin pad
   B. Heat lamp
   C. Bed board
   D. Cradle

16. The physician has ordered warm saline dressings to be applied to Mr. Dine's heel ulcer for 20 minutes twice a day. A nurse observes another staff nurse preparing a clean basin and a washcloth to carry out the treatment. Which of these approaches by the nurse who makes the observation would be APPROPRIATE? 16.___
    A. Interrupt the nurse assembling supplies to discuss the procedure
    B. Present the situation for discussion at a team conference
    C. Do nothing, as the procedure is being done using correct technique
    D. Do nothing, as each nurse is accountable for her or his own actions

17. Mr. Dine's lesions have not responded to conservative medical therapy. He is scheduled to have a below-the-knee amputation of the affected extremity. Mr. Dine's orders include administration of regular insulin on a sliding scale. Mr. Dine, who received isophane (NPH) insulin prior to his admission to the hospital, has been on regular insulin since admission. Regular insulin is to be continued for him until after his recovery from surgery. Mr. Dine asks what the reason is for this order. Which of the following information would give Mr. Dine the BEST explanation? 17.___
    A. When complications are present, diabetes is more manageable with regular insulin.
    B. During the first week after a patient recovers from an episode of diabetic acidosis, the likelihood of a recurrence is greatest.
    C. Diminished activity intensifies the body's response to long-acting insulin.
    D. Diabetic acidosis causes a temporary increase in the rate of food absorption.

18. Mr. Dine asks why he cannot be given insulin by mouth. He should be informed that insulin is NOT given by mouth because it 18.___
    A. is destroyed by digestive enzymes
    B. is irritating to the gastrointestinal tract
    C. is detoxified by the liver
    D. cannot be regulated as it is absorbed

19. Mr. Dine is receiving an intravenous infusion of 5% glucose in distilled water. Regular insulin is administered intravenously every two hours. The purpose of the insulin is to 19.___
    A. enhance carbohydrate metabolism
    B. promote conversion of fat to glycogen
    C. stimulate gluconeogenesis
    D. assist in the regulation of fluid absorption

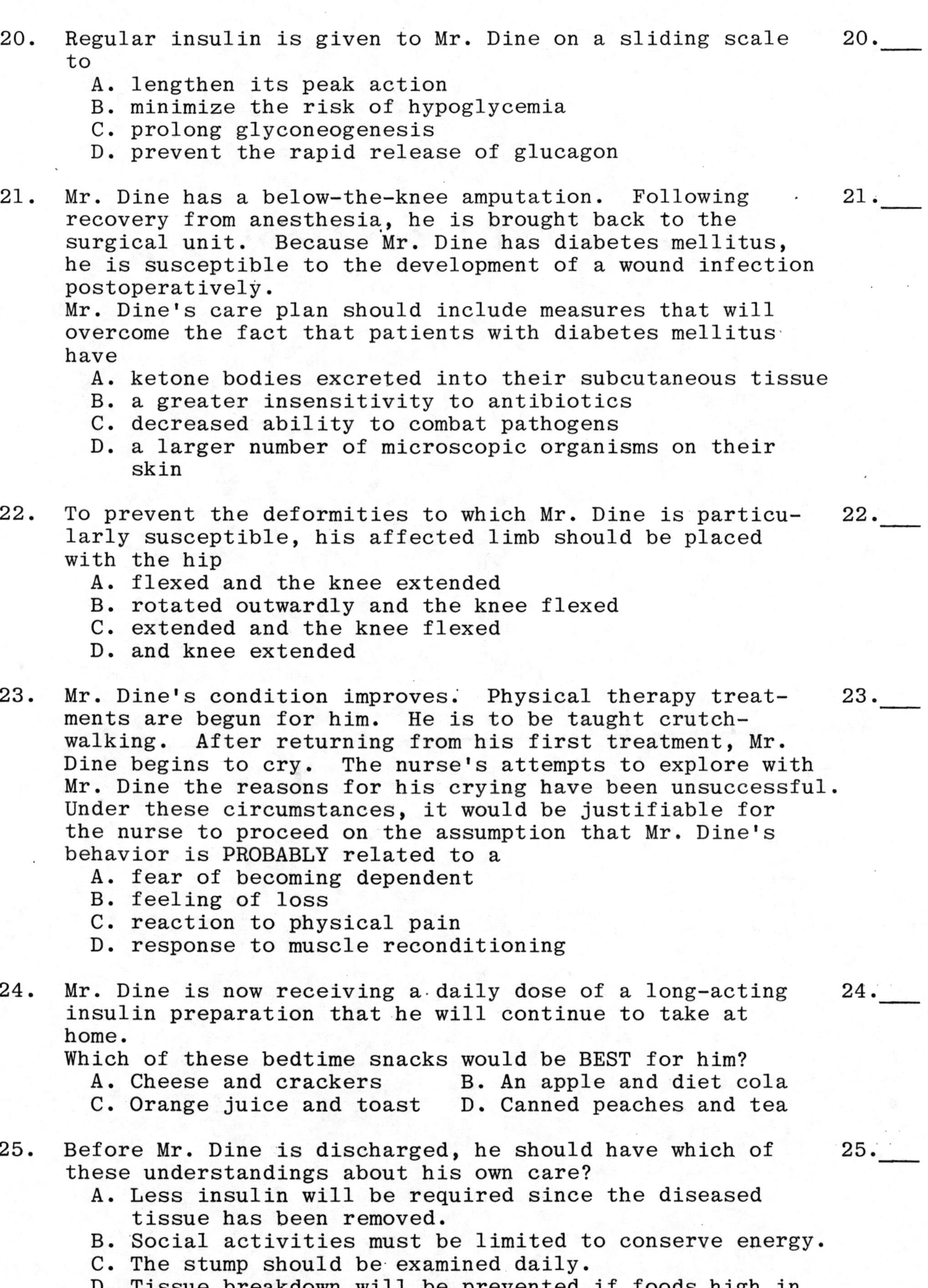

20. Regular insulin is given to Mr. Dine on a sliding scale to 20.___
   A. lengthen its peak action
   B. minimize the risk of hypoglycemia
   C. prolong glyconeogenesis
   D. prevent the rapid release of glucagon

21. Mr. Dine has a below-the-knee amputation. Following recovery from anesthesia, he is brought back to the surgical unit. Because Mr. Dine has diabetes mellitus, he is susceptible to the development of a wound infection postoperatively. 21.___
Mr. Dine's care plan should include measures that will overcome the fact that patients with diabetes mellitus have
   A. ketone bodies excreted into their subcutaneous tissue
   B. a greater insensitivity to antibiotics
   C. decreased ability to combat pathogens
   D. a larger number of microscopic organisms on their skin

22. To prevent the deformities to which Mr. Dine is particularly susceptible, his affected limb should be placed with the hip 22.___
   A. flexed and the knee extended
   B. rotated outwardly and the knee flexed
   C. extended and the knee flexed
   D. and knee extended

23. Mr. Dine's condition improves. Physical therapy treatments are begun for him. He is to be taught crutch-walking. After returning from his first treatment, Mr. Dine begins to cry. The nurse's attempts to explore with Mr. Dine the reasons for his crying have been unsuccessful. Under these circumstances, it would be justifiable for the nurse to proceed on the assumption that Mr. Dine's behavior is PROBABLY related to a 23.___
   A. fear of becoming dependent
   B. feeling of loss
   C. reaction to physical pain
   D. response to muscle reconditioning

24. Mr. Dine is now receiving a daily dose of a long-acting insulin preparation that he will continue to take at home. 24.___
Which of these bedtime snacks would be BEST for him?
   A. Cheese and crackers B. An apple and diet cola
   C. Orange juice and toast D. Canned peaches and tea

25. Before Mr. Dine is discharged, he should have which of these understandings about his own care? 25.___
   A. Less insulin will be required since the diseased tissue has been removed.
   B. Social activities must be limited to conserve energy.
   C. The stump should be examined daily.
   D. Tissue breakdown will be prevented if foods high in vitamin C are taken daily.

KEY (CORRECT ANSWERS)

1. C
2. B
3. A
4. C
5. D
6. A
7. A
8. A
9. A
10. A
11. C
12. D
13. B
14. C
15. D
16. A
17. A
18. A
19. A
20. B
21. C
22. D
23. B
24. A
25. C

TEST 3

DIRECTIONS: Each question or incomplete statement is followed by several suggested answers or completions. Select the one that BEST answers the question or completes the statement. *PRINT THE LETTER OF THE CORRECT ANSWER IN THE SPACE AT THE RIGHT.*

1. A physician orders the following pre-operative medications for a child: Demerol hydrochloride 8 mg.; Atropine sulfate 0.06 mg. On hand are the following vials: Meperidine (Demerol) hydrochloride 50 mg. in 1 cc.; Atropine sulfate 0.40 mg. in 1 cc. In order to administer the prescribed doses, the nurse should give _____ of meperidine and _____ of atropine. 1.___
   A. 0.16 cc.; 0.15 cc. B. 0.26 cc.; 0.20 cc.
   C. 1 minim; 3 minims D. 2 minims; 4 minims

2. To provide care to a patient who has lost a body part or valued function, which of these measures is ESSENTIAL to include in the care plan? 2.___
   A. Inviting the assistance of a person who has a similar handicap
   B. Encouraging an immediate independence in self-care
   C. Providing information to the patient about available prosthetic devices
   D. Allowing adequate time for the patient to work through his grief

Questions 3-9.

DIRECTIONS: Questions 3 through 9 are to be answered on the basis of the following information.

Ms. Gloria Goldstein, 40 years old, visits a physician because of pain in her left leg. The physician determines that Ms. Goldstein has thrombophlebitis in her left leg and hospital admission is arranged. Her orders include bed rest and bishydroxycoumarin (Dicumarol).

3. Bed rest is prescribed for Ms. Goldstein in order to 3.___
   A. promote fluctuations in the venous pressure of both extremities
   B. improve the capacity of the venous circulation in both extremities
   C. minimize the potential for release of a thrombus in the affected extremity
   D. prevent thrombus formation in the unaffected extremity

4. The EXPECTED action of Dicumarol is to 4.___
   A. dissolve a thrombus
   B. prevent extension of a thrombus
   C. promote healing of the infarction
   D. reduce vascular necrosis

5. To detect a common untoward effect of Dicumarol, the nurse should assess Ms. Goldstein for the possible development of 5.___
   A. generalized dermatitis B. hematuria
   C. urinary retention D. vitamin K deficiency

6. While Ms. Goldstein is receiving Dicumarol, she should be monitored by which of these laboratory tests? 6.___
   A. Prothrombin time B. Clotting time
   C. Red cell fragility D. Platelet count

7. An order for which of these medications should be questioned because it is usually contraindicated for a patient receiving Dicumarol? 7.___
   A. Cortisone
   B. Aspirin
   C. Chlorpromazine hydrochloride (Thorazine)
   D. Isoproterenol (Isuprel) hydrochloride

8. The nurse is talking with Ms. Goldstein on the third day of her hospitalization. Suddenly, Ms. Goldstein, who is in bed, complains of a sharp pain in the left side of her chest. The physician establishes a diagnosis of pulmonary embolus. Ms. Goldstein's orders include absolute bed rest and heparin. 8.___
   Which of these medications should be READILY available while Ms. Goldstein is receiving heparin therapy?
   A. Procainamide (Pronestyl) hydrochloride
   B. Protamine sulfate
   C. Papaverine hydrochloride
   D. Calcium gluconate

9. At lunchtime one day, Ms. Goldstein, who is on a regular diet, states that she does not feel hungry. 9.___
   The nurse should
   A. encourage her to eat the full meal
   B. emphasize her need for protein
   C. limit her snacks
   D. allow her to eat as she likes

10. The BEST beginning point in offering support to a patient in time of crisis is to 10.___
   A. tell the client what to do to solve the problem
   B. imply that the client is a competent person
   C. find a person or agency to take care of the problem
   D. remind the client that everyone has to cope with crises

Questions 11-16.

DIRECTIONS: Questions 11 through 16 are to be answered on the basis of the following information.

Ms. Sylvia Capp, 53 years old, has a physical examination, and it is determined that she is hypertensive. She attends the medical clinic and is receiving health instruction and supervision. Ms. Capp is to receive a thiazide drug and a diet low in fat, sodium, and triglycerides.

11. The finding that would constitute a significant index of hypertension is a 11.___
  A. pulse deficit of 10 beats per minute
  B. regular pulse of 90 beats per minute
  C. systolic pressure fluctuating between 150 and 160 mm. Hg.
  D. sustained diastolic pressure greater than 90 mm. Hg.

12. The nurse asks Ms. Capp to select foods that best meet her diet prescription. 12.___
Ms. Capp's knowledge of goods lowest in both fat and sodium would be ACCURATE if she selected
  A. tossed salad with blue cheese dressing, cold cuts, and vanilla cookies
  B. split pea soup, cheese sandwich, and a banana
  C. cold baked chicken, lettuce with sliced tomatoes, and applesauce
  D. beans and frankfurters, carrot and celery sticks, and a plain cupcake

13. When teaching Ms. Capp about her diet, the nurse should include which of these instructions? 13.___
  A. Avoid eating canned fruits
  B. Season your meat with lemon juice or vinegar
  C. Restrict your intake of green vegetables
  D. Drink diet soda instead of decaffeinated coffee

14. To assist Ms. Capp to comply with a low-fat diet, the information about fats that would be MOST useful to her is the 14.___
  A. amount of fat in processed meats
  B. method of preparing foods to limit the fat content
  C. comparison of hydrogenated fats to emulsified fats
  D. caloric differences of foods containing fats and carbohydrates

15. Because Ms. Capp is receiving a thiazide drug, her diet should include foods that are high in 15.___
  A. calcium B. potassium
  C. iron D. magnesium

16. Ms. Capp tells the nurse that she smokes two packs of cigarettes a day. 16.___
To initiate a plan that will assist Ms. Capp in overcoming her smoking habit, which of these actions by the nurse would probably be MOST effective?
   A. Have her identify those times when she feels that she must have a cigarette
   B. Ask her to describe what she knows about the deleterious effects of smoking on her condition
   C. Explain to her how smoking contributes to environmental pollution
   D. Impress on her the realization that smoking is a form of addiction that is no longer socially acceptable

Questions 17-25.

DIRECTIONS: Questions 17 through 25 are to be answered on the basis of the following information.

Mr. Ethan Allen, 46 years old, is admitted to a center for the treatment of persons who abuse alcohol. He had been drinking a quart or more of liquor a day for 10 to 15 years. He was drinking up to the time of his admission. His wife is with him.

17. Mr. Allen's immediate treatment is MOST likely to include orders for 17.___
   A. oral fluids, ascorbic acid, and a narcotic
   B. a cool bath, a barbiturate, and blood lithium level
   C. full diet as tolerated, thiamine, and a tranquilizer
   D. a spinal tap, bromides, and restraints

18. If Mr. Allen develops delirium tremens, which of these environmental factors is likely to be MOST disturbing? 18.___
   A. Strangers
   B. Shadows
   C. Unfamiliar procedures
   D. Medicinal odors

19. Ms. Allen says to the nurse, *I'd do anything to help my husband stop drinking.* 19.___
The PRIMARY goal of the nurse's response should be to
   A. get Ms. Allen to clarify the problem as she sees it
   B. have Ms. Allen join Al-Anon
   C. tell Ms. Allen that she has done all she could to help her husband
   D. have Ms. Allen understand that alcoholism is a problem that only her husband can solve

20. In giving care to Mr. Allen, the nurse should be alert for complications of withdrawal, which include 20.___
   A. aphasia
   B. hypotension
   C. diarrhea
   D. convulsions

21. After several weeks of group therapy, Mr. Allen says to the nurse, *I've never been able to face life without alcohol.* 21.___
Which of the responses would initially be MOST appropriate?
   A. I know how you feel, Mr. Allen. We all have difficulty in meeting some problems.
   B. But now you know where to go for help.
   C. Perhaps you can manage if you join Alcoholics Anonymous, Mr. Allen.
   D. That has been the way you have dealt with your problems.

22. Mr. Allen's success in abstaining from drinking is thought to depend on his 22.___
   A. admission that his behavior is detrimental to himself and his family
   B. conviction that he must change and has some capacity for change
   C. ability to express remorse
   D. having taken a pledge witnessed by fellow alcoholics

23. Mr. Allen is started on disulfiram (Antabuse), which he will continue to take after discharge from the hospital. It should be emphasized to Mr. Allen that while he is on Antabuse, he must NEVER take 23.___
   A. elixir of terpin hydrate
   B. aspirin
   C. bicarbonate of soda
   D. antihistamines

24. Patients such as Mr. Allen may develop Korsakoff's psychosis. 24.___
Which of these symptoms is associated with this condition?
   A. Fantastic delusions and fear
   B. Sullenness and suspiciousness
   C. Amnesia and confabulation
   D. Nihilistic ideas and tearfulness

25. The nurse explains Alcoholics Anonymous to Mr. Allen. An understanding implemented by Alcoholics Anonymous is that people 25.___
   A. feel less alone when they feel understood
   B. are more likely to be able to handle problems when they are alerted to them ahead of time
   C. are dependent upon their environment for cues that keep them oriented
   D. resort to defense mechanisms as a means of coping with anxiety

---

KEY (CORRECT ANSWERS)

1. A
2. D
3. C
4. B
5. B
6. A
7. B
8. B
9. D
10. B
11. D
12. C
13. B
14. B
15. B
16. A
17. C
18. B
19. A
20. D
21. D
22. B
23. A
24. C
25. A

EXAMINATION SECTION

TEST 1

DIRECTIONS: Each question or incomplete statement is followed by several suggested answers or completions. Select the one that BEST answers the question or completes the statement. *PRINT THE LETTER OF THE CORRECT ANSWER IN THE SPACE AT THE RIGHT.*

Questions 1-3.

DIRECTIONS: Questions 1 through 3 are to be answered on the basis of the following information.

Anna comes in with a variety of vague complaints over the past 8 months. The physician suspects multiple sclerosis.

1. The MOST common initial symptom associated with multiple sclerosis is 1.___
   A. diplopia; blurred vision
   B. diarrhea
   C. dementia
   D. dermatitis

2. Anna, when the diagnosis of MS is confirmed, feels very upset and asks if she is going to die. 2.___
   The nurse should reply:
   A. Most individuals live a normal life span
   B. Ask the doctor
   C. Everyone has to die one day
   D. Prognosis is variable with remissions and exacerbations

3. Anna complains of urinary urgency and frequency. 3.___
   What should be the INITIAL nursing measure?
   A. Palpatate the supra pubic area to assess if the symptoms are caused by a full bladder
   B. Monitor urinary output
   C. Limit fluids
   D. All of the above

Questions 4-5.

DIRECTIONS: Questions 4 and 5 are to be answered on the basis of the following information.

Mary fractured her left hip as a result of falling on the doorstep. A fractured hip and osteoporosis are confirmed by x-ray.

4. The change in the x-ray due to osteoporosis which is MOST easily observable is 4.___
   A. compression fractures of vertebrae
   B. long bones
   C. facial bones
   D. joints of hands and feet

5. In order to limit the further progression of osteoporosis, the nurse should advise Mary to 5.___
   A. increase consumption of milk
   B. take supplemental calcium and vitamin D
   C. increase consumption of eggs
   D. take supplemental vitamin E

Questions 6-11.

DIRECTIONS: Questions 6 through 11 are to be answered on the basis of the following information.

Mr. Thompson is admitted for diagnosis and treatment of a lesion in the right lung. A bronchoscopy is performed.

6. The nurse should withhold food and fluids for several hours to prevent 6.___
   A. abdominal pain
   B. dyspepsia
   C. dysphagia
   D. aspiration of food

7. Mr. Thompson is diagnosed with lung cancer, and pneumonectomy is performed. The physician orders IV fluids at 80 ml/hour. 7.___
   To adjust the drip rate, the nurse must know the
   A. drops per milliliter delivered by the infusion set-up
   B. total volume in the IV bag
   C. diameter of tubing used
   D. size of needle or catheter in vein

8. On the first post-operative day, Mr. Thompson suddenly sits up in bed. His respiration is labored, and he is making a crowing sound. He seems very pale. 8.___
   The nurse should
   A. notify the physician
   B. auscultate the left lung
   C. check the tube for patency
   D. provide warm blankets

9. The BEST position that Mr. Thompson can use for lying which would permit good ventilation is the _____ position. 9.___
   A. supine or right lying
   B. supine or left lying
   C. Fowler's
   D. all of the above

10. Irradiation is prescribed for Mr. Thompson on an out-patient basis. 10.____
The nurse should tell Mr. Thompson how to take care of his skin and should EMPHASIZE
A. frequent washings
B. massaging 4-7 times to increase circulation
C. keeping skin dry and protecting from abrasions
D. all of the above

11. In order to prevent vitamin D toxicity, Mr. Thompson should AVOID eating 11.____
A. fruit and eggnog
B. cottage cheese
C. milk products and whole milk
D. all of the above

12. _____ are at INCREASED risk for developing gall bladder disease. 12.____
A. Females under age 40 with a family history of gall-stones
B. Males under age 40 with a past history of hepatitis
C. Females over age 40 who are obese
D. Males over age 40 who have low serum cholesterol

13. Which of the following is TRUE regarding an oral chole-cystogram done for a diagnosis of gallstones? 13.____
A. The test is given on 1 day and it must be repeated if the results are inconclusive.
B. A low fat dinner is given so that large amounts of bile will be stored in the gallbladder on the day of the test.
C. The contrast medium in the pills often causes diarrhea.
D. All of the above

14. The MOST important dietary modification in a patient before cholecystectomy is to be performed is 14.____
A. eating low cholesterol foods to avoid formation of gallstones
B. eating soft-textured foods to aid digestion
C. reducing fats to avoid stimulation of the cholecysto-kinin mechanism for bile release
D. increasing proteins to promote tissue healing

Questions 15-19.

DIRECTIONS: Questions 15 through 19 are to be answered on the basis of the following information.

Mr. Dillon is admitted to the hospital for a fever of unknown origin. He recently experienced an unexplained weight loss and a series of respiratory infections. Mr. Dillon is accompanied by Mr. Jordan, who is his life partner. AIDS-related complex is suspected.

15. An AIDS diagnosis is based on a positive HIV antibody test and 15.___
    A. a history of weight loss
    B. a history of very high fevers
    C. the presence of an associated opportunistic infection
    D. a positive ELISA test

16. When taking Mr. Dillon's blood pressure, the nurse MUST 16.___
    A. wear gloves
    B. wear mask and gown
    C. wash hands thoroughly
    D. none of the above

17. Mr. Dillon is receiving AZT. 17.___
The MOST important thing for the nurse to monitor is
    A. complete blood cell count
    B. serum electrolytes
    C. cardiac enzymes
    D. liver enzymes

18. It is important for the nurse to monitor complete blood count for Mr. Dillon because AZT causes 18.___
    A. anemia
    B. leukopenia
    C. granulocytopenia
    D. all of the above

19. The difference between AIDS and AIDS-related complex (ARC) is that ARC is 19.___
    A. more physiologically debilitating
    B. not transmitted by blood contact
    C. not associated with opportunistic infection
    D. not infective to other persons

Questions 20-25.

DIRECTIONS: Questions 20 through 25 are to be answered on the basis of the following information.

Mr. Burton is admitted to the hospital with severe left flank pain, nausea, and hematuria. Ureteral calculus is suspected.

20. What should be the FIRST nursing action after admission? 20.___
    A. Increase fluid intake
    B. Administer prescribed analgesics
    C. Obtain urine for urinalysis
    D. Obtain urine for culture and sensitivity

21. The type of pain MOST likely described by Mr. Burton to lead to a diagnosis of ureteral calculus is 21.___
    A. boring pain in the flank
    B. pain intensified on micturation
    C. spasmodic pain on the left side radiating to the suprapubis
    D. constant pain in the costovertebral angle

22. To prepare for an intravenous pyelogram to be done the next morning, the nurse should advise Mr. Burton to 22.___
   A. omit dinner the night before
   B. take a laxative before going to bed
   C. take a fat-free dinner
   D. stop all liquids

23. The intravenous pyelogram confirmed the presence of a stone. 23.___
If Mr. Burton's blood test indicated elevated purine instead of calcium, then the stone would PROBABLY be composed of
   A. struvite
   B. oxalate
   C. cystine
   D. uric acid

24. By the next day, Mr. Burton's urinary output is much less than his intake. 24.___
If his bladder is NOT distended, then the nurse should suspect
   A. oliguria
   B. renal failure
   C. hydroureter
   D. all of the above

25. A ureterolithotomy was performed on Mr. Burton. 25.___
Signs and symptoms of urinary tract infections of which Mr. Burton should be made aware before being discharged include
   A. urgency and frequency of urination
   B. burning on urination
   C. fever
   D. all of the above

KEY (CORRECT ANSWERS)

1. A
2. D
3. A
4. A
5. B

6. D
7. A
8. B
9. A
10. C

11. D
12. C
13. D
14. C
15. C

16. C
17. A
18. D
19. C
20. B

21. C
22. B
23. D
24. C
25. D

TEST 2

DIRECTIONS: Each question or incomplete statement is followed by several suggested answers or completions. Select the one that BEST answers the question or completes the statement. *PRINT THE LETTER OF THE CORRECT ANSWER IN THE SPACE AT THE RIGHT.*

Questions 1-2.

DIRECTIONS: Questions 1 and 2 are to be answered on the basis of the following information.

Mr. Wilson, who has a 25-year history of excessive alcohol consumption, is admitted to the hospital with jaundice and acites.

1. What nursing action is MOST important in the first 48 hours after admission? 1.___
   A. Increase fluid intake
   B. Improve nutritional status
   C. Monitor vital signs
   D. Prepare for rehabilitative therapy

2. Mr. Wilson complains of severe pruritis. In order to relieve this, the physician would PROBABLY suggest 2.___
   A. sponge baths with alcohol
   B. application of baby oil
   C. application of cold cream
   D. baths with sodium bicarbonate solution

3. The typical gait associated with Parkinson's disease is referred to as 3.___
   A. ataxic
   B. spastic
   C. scissoring
   D. shuffling

4. While performing a physical examination and taking the history of a patient of Parkinson's disease, the nurse should assess the patient for 4.___
   A. hyperextension of the neck
   B. low-pitched, monotonous voice
   C. frequent bouts of diarrhea
   D. recent increase in appetite

5. Common signs and symptoms of Parkinson's disease include 5.___
   A. characteristic masked facies
   B. non-intention tremor
   C. constipation
   D. all of the above

6. Side effects related to levodopa include 6.___
   A. anorexia B. tachycardia
   C. nausea D. all of the above

7. In patients receiving heparin therapy, there is always potential for hemorrhage. 7.___
   The nurse in such a case should be ready to administer
   A. vitamin K B. warfarin
   C. protamine sulphate D. panheparin

Questions 8-11.

DIRECTIONS: Questions 8 through 11 are to be answered on the basis of the following information.

Mr. Foster is admitted to the hospital for repair of bilateral inguinal hernias under general anesthesia.

8. Before surgery, the nurse should look for signs of strangulation of hernias. 8.___
   An EARLY sign of strangulation would be
   A. projectile vomiting B. sharp abdominal pain
   C. increased flatus D. decreased bowel sounds

9. Pre-operatively, the nurse should teach Mr. Foster how to _____, as he will have to do it post-operatively. 9.___
   A. perform coughing and deep breathing exercises
   B. turn and change his position every 2 hours
   C. have a nasogastric tube in his nose
   D. all of the above

10. After the bilateral herniorrhaphy, Mr. Foster should be observed for the development of 10.___
    A. a hydrocele B. urinary retention
    C. paralytic ileus D. thrombophlebitis

11. If Mr. Foster's scrotum becomes swollen, the nurse should 11.___
    A. assist him with a sitz bath
    B. apply warm soaks to the scrotum
    C. prepare for incision and drainage
    D. elevate the scrotum using soft support

12. Mrs. McDonald, a 62 year-old obese woman, comes in complaining of being tired all the time. Her tests reveal hyperglycemia. She is diagnosed with type II diabetes. 12.___
    The nurse should expect Mrs. McDonald's lab values to reveal
    A. ketones in blood but not in urine
    B. urine negative for ketones but 4+ glucose
    C. urine and blood positive for glucose and ketones
    D. glucose in urine but not in blood

Questions 13-15.

DIRECTIONS: Questions 13 through 15 are to be answered on the basis of the following information.

Mrs. Eastwood, who is 65 years old, comes in with a complaint of painful swelling of the distal joint of her ring finger. A tentative diagnosis of rheumatoid arthritis is made.

13. Mrs. Eastwood is confused because her lab tests were negative, and she asks if she *really* has this arthritis. The BEST reply by the nurse would be: 13.___
   A. Don't think about it
   B. Eventually the tests will be positive
   C. Lab tests are often negative in the early stage
   D. None of the above

14. Mrs. Eastwood returns for the lab check and tells the nurse that she feels much better because she had been using aspirin, but she still feels a ringing in her ears. This may be due to 14.___
   A. the aging process
   B. cerumen in the ear
   C. involvement of the 8th cranial nerve because of aspirin
   D. otitis media

15. Mrs. Eastwood asks if she should take vitamins. The nurse's BEST response would be: 15.___
   A. Absolutely, they are good for you
   B. Older people need them badly
   C. There is no evidence that healthy older people require added vitamin supplements
   D. When you start vitamins, cut down on food

16. A patient with fatigue, shortness of breath, and swelling of hands has a history of rheumatic fever. On auscultation of this patient, you would expect the Si (first heart sound) to be LOUDEST at the 16.___
   A. right lateral border
   B. apex of the heart
   C. left lateral border
   D. base of the heart

17. When taking a history of a patient with glaucoma, the nurse should expect the complaint of 17.___
   A. seeing floating specks
   B. flashes of light
   C. loss of peripheral vision
   D. intolerance to light

18. The type of eye drop MOST commonly used in caring for a patient with glaucoma is 18.___
   A. pilocarpine
   B. atropine sulphate
   C. cyclopentolate
   D. tetracaine

Questions 19-23.

DIRECTIONS: Questions 19 through 23 are to be answered on the basis of the following information.

Susan, 47 years old, develops acute glomerulonephritis following a streptococcal infection.

19. During assessment, the nurse should expect Susan to report a history of 19.___
   A. recent weight loss B. mild headaches
   C. nocturia D. increased appetite

20. To prevent future attacks of glomerulonephritis, the nurse should instruct Susan to 20.___
   A. continue restrictions on fluid intake
   B. avoid physical activity
   C. seek treatment of any respiratory infection
   D. none of the above

21. Susan had extensive scarring and finally developed chronic renal failure. She is scheduled for a kidney transplant. After the transplant, the nurse should measure Susan's urinary output every 21.___
   A. 15 minutes B. 30 minutes
   C. hour D. 2 hours

22. The MOST important determinant that Susan's new kidney is functioning properly is 22.___
   A. white blood cell count B. serum creatinine
   C. renal scan D. 24 hour output

23. Signs of rejection of a transplant kidney include 23.___
   A. increased urine output B. elevated blood pressure
   C. weight loss D. subnormal temperature

Questions 24-25.

DIRECTIONS: Questions 24 and 25 are to be answered on the basis of the following information.

A 26 year-old college student is admitted to the hospital with a history of severe cramping and violent diarrhea of 2 days duration. A tentative diagnosis of salmonellosis is made.

24. Enteric precautions for salmonellosis include 24.___
   A. double bagging laundry B. wearing masks
   C. isolation D. limiting visiting hours

25. The diagnosis of salmonella is confirmed by 25.___
A. CBC
B. urinalysis
C. febrile agglutinin test
D. stool culture

KEY (CORRECT ANSWERS)

1. C
2. D
3. D
4. B
5. D

6. D
7. C
8. B
9. A
10. B

11. D
12. B
13. C
14. C
15. C

16. B
17. C
18. A
19. B
20. C

21. C
22. B
23. B
24. A
25. D

EXAMINATION SECTION
TEST 1

DIRECTIONS: Each question or incomplete statement is followed by several suggested answers or completions. Select the one that BEST answers the question or completes the statement. *PRINT THE LETTER OF THE CORRECT ANSWER IN THE SPACE AT THE RIGHT.*

Questions 1-10.

DIRECTIONS: Questions 1 through 10 are to be answered on the basis of the following information.

Fifty year-old George Hoffman works in the basement of a garment factory. All of a sudden, he starts losing consciousness. An ambulance is called, and he is taken to the emergency room of the nearest hospital.

During the initial examination in the emergency room, he is found to have rapid, shallow breathing, non-palpable pulses over major vessels, and absent heart sounds.

1. Of the following, the MOST likely nursing diagnosis for this patient is 1.___
   A. arteriosclerosis
   B. cardiopulmonary arrest
   C. restrictive cardiomyopathy
   D. endocarditis

2. The nursing intervention of HIGHEST priority after receiving George in the emergency room would be 2.___
   A. to administer dopamine and norepinephrine to treat for shock
   B. to administer calcium chloride to help heartbeat
   C. defibrillation
   D. CPR

3. All of the following would be part of George's drug therapy EXCEPT 3.___
   A. lidocaine and procainamide
   B. epinephrine
   C. penicillin G
   D. sodium bicarbonate

4. While assessing George, the nurse probably does NOT expect to notice 4.___
   A. pallor B. dilation of pupils
   C. ventricular fibrillation D. petechiae and edema

5. George is unconscious. In an unconscious person, the relaxed tongue and neck muscles fail to lift the tongue from the posterior pharyngeal wall, blocking the hypopharyngeal airway. The nurse applies a basic head tilt maneuver to open the patient's airway, but does not receive a positive response.
Additional measures which may then be used by the nurse to open the airway include 5.___
   A. head tilt-chin lift
   B. head tilt-neck lift
   C. mandibular jaw thrust
   D. all of the above

6. George is also found to have suffered cervical spine injury as a result of falling.
The nurse should know that _____ is absolutely contraindicated in the presence of cervical spine injury. 6.___
   A. direct current defibrillation
   B. external cardiac compression
   C. backward head tilt
   D. all of the above

7. In single-rescuer CPR, the nurse would give 2 breaths (1 to 1.5 sec. each) after each cycle of _____ cardiac compressions, delivered at a rate of 80 to 100/minute. 7.___
   A. 5   B. 10   C. 15   D. 20

8. All of the following would be important and appropriate nursing interventions to save George's life EXCEPT: 8.___
   A. Begin precordial thump and, if successful, administer calcium chloride
   B. If precordial thump is unsuccessful, perform defibrillation
   C. If defibrillation is unsuccessful, initiate CPR immediately
   D. Assist with administration of and monitor effects of additional emergency drugs

9. In 2-rescuer CPR, one ventilation (1.5 to 2 sec.) should be given after each cycle of _____ cardiac compressions, delivered at a rate of 80 to 100/minute. 9.___
   A. 5   B. 10   C. 15   D. 20

10. Which of the following drugs is used as the standard therapy for ventricular fibrillation (VF) or ventricular tachycardia (VT), and is used with countershock to convert VF? 10.___
   A. Procainamide   B. Bretylium tosylate
   C. Lidocaine   D. Epinephrine

Questions 11-20.

DIRECTIONS: Questions 11 through 20 are to be answered on the basis of the following information.

52 year-old John Goodman is brought to the emergency room by his wife with complaints of fever, cough, upper quadrant pain, and joint pain. Mrs. Goodman informs the health care team that John has also been losing weight.

11. John has been diagnosed with infective endocarditis. Mrs. Goodman has no knowledge about this disease, so she anxiously asks the nurse about it. 11.___
The nurse explains to Mrs. Goodman that infective endocarditis is a(n)
   A. inflammation of the parietal pericardium caused by a viral infection
   B. accumulation of fluid in the pericardium that prevents adequate ventricular filling, caused by a fungal infection
   C. microbial infection of the endocardium which may result in valvular incompetence or obstruction, myocardial abscess, or mycotic aneurysm
   D. formation of platelet and fibrin thrombi on cardiac valves and the adjacent endocardium in response to bacterial infection

12. Which of the following bacterias is among the common causes of infection in endocarditis? 12.___
   A. S. aureus
   B. S. viridans
   C. B. hemolytic streptococcus and gonococcus
   D. All of the above

13. While assessing John, the nurse expects to find all of the following EXCEPT 13.___
   A. malaise and fatigue
   B. edema
   C. elevated WBC and ESR
   D. increased Hgb and Hct

14. As a clinical manifestation, the symptom found in John that is NOT secondary to emboli is _____ pain. 14.___
   A. upper left quadrant
   B. flank
   C. joint
   D. chest

15. All of the following medications will be part of John's drug therapy EXCEPT 15.___
   A. epinephrine, to enhance endocardial contractile force
   B. antibiotics specific to the sensitivity of the organism cultured
   C. penicillin G and streptomycin, if the organism is not known
   D. antipyretics

16. In order for John to maintain homeostasis and avoid complications over long-term hospitalization, the one of the following things a nurse does NOT have to do is 16.___
   A. administer antibiotics as ordered
   B. control temperature elevation by administration of antipyretics
   C. evaluate for complications of emboli and congestive heart failure
   D. record baseline blood pressure in three positions, i.e., lying, sitting, and standing, in both arms

17. To isolate the etiologic agent, the nurse would perform _____ blood cultures of _____ mL each within 24 hours. 17.___
   A. 1 to 3; 10 to 20   B. 3 to 5; 20 to 30
   C. 5 to 7; 10 to 20   D. 3 to 5; 15 to 20

18. All of the following factors are associated with poor prognosis of infective endocarditis EXCEPT 18.___
   A. heart failure
   B. delay in initiating therapy
   C. young age
   D. major embolic events

19. Even after successful antimicrobial therapy, John will be at risk of sterile emboli and valve rupture for 19.___
   A. 6 months   B. 1 year   C. 1½ years   D. 2 years

20. John has recovered and is now ready to be discharged from the hospital. 20.___
While discussing discharge planning, the nurse would instruct John and his wife regarding all of the following EXCEPT
   A. types of procedures or treatments that increase the chances of recurrence
   B. antifungal therapy, including name, purpose, dose, frequency, and side effects
   C. signs and symptoms of recurrent endocarditis
   D. avoidance of individuals with known infections

Questions 21-30.

DIRECTIONS: Questions 21 through 30 are to be answered on the basis of the following information.

54 year-old Donna Smith is brought to the hospital's emergency room by her husband after having fever, malaise, and chest pain aggravated by breathing and swallowing.

21. After being examined by the physician, Donna is diagnosed with pericarditis. Mr. Smith asks the nurse about the nature of this disease. 21.___
The nurse tells him that pericarditis is

A. an accumulation of fluid or blood in the pericardium that prevents adequate ventricular filling, caused by a fungal infection
B. an inflammation of the visceral and parietal pericardium, caused by a bacterial, viral, or fungal infection
C. the formation of platelet and fibrin thrombi on cardiac valves and the adjacent pericardium in response to bacterial infection
D. none of the above

22. Acute pericarditis may be a manifestation of all of the following EXCEPT 22.___
A. rheumatoid arthritis
B. systemic lupus erythematosus
C. hemochromatosis
D. scleroderma

23. Commonly used drugs that may produce acute pericarditis do NOT include 23.___
A. procainamide
B. hydralazine
C. isoniazid
D. lidocaine

24. Common causes of pericarditis include 24.___
A. tuberculosis
B. streptococcal infections
C. staphylococcal infection
D. all of the above

25. A scratchy, leathery sound heard in both systole and diastole is the CLASSIC sign of acute pericarditis known as 25.___
A. pericardial friction rub
B. epicardial rub friction
C. myocardial friction rub
D. dip and plateau

26. During Donna's assessment, the nurse does NOT expect to notice 26.___
A. cough and hemoptysis
B. tachycardia and pulsus paradoxus
C. cyanosis or pallor
D. decreased WBC and ESR

27. Which of the following is INCORRECT regarding Donna's drug therapy? 27.___
It
A. is medication for pain relief
B. includes corticosteroids, salicylates, and indomethacin
C. includes calcium chloride
D. is specific antibiotic therapy against the causative organism

28. The FALSE statement regarding chronic pericarditis is: 28.___
   A. It may be serous, fibrous, adhesive, hemorrhagic, purulent, fibrinous, or calcific
   B. It is asymptomatic unless constrictive pericarditis is present
   C. Coagulants are usually contraindicated in pericardial disease
   D. As a general treatment, meperidine 50 to 100 mg orally or IM may be given q 4 hours for pain

29. All of the following are proper nursing interventions to control Donna's condition EXCEPT 29.___
   A. ensuring comfort: bedrest with semi or high-Fowler's position
   B. monitoring hemodynamic parameters carefully
   C. administering medications as ordered and monitoring effects
   D. assessing for vascular complications

30. Donna has recovered and is now ready to be discharged. During the discharge planning conference, the nurse would probably NOT advise Mr. and Mrs. Smith about 30.___
   A. signs and symptoms of pericarditis indicative of a recurrence
   B. medication regimen including name, purpose, dosage, frequency, and side effects
   C. keeping all the emergency medications available at all times
   D. none of the above

KEY (CORRECT ANSWERS)

1. B	11. C	21. B
2. D	12. D	22. C
3. C	13. D	23. D
4. D	14. C	24. D
5. D	15. A	25. A
6. C	16. D	26. D
7. C	17. B	27. C
8. A	18. C	28. C
9. A	19. B	29. D
10. C	20. B	30. A

TEST 2

DIRECTIONS: Each question or incomplete statement is followed by several suggested answers or completions. Select the one that BEST answers the question or completes the statement. *PRINT THE LETTER OF THE CORRECT ANSWER IN THE SPACE AT THE RIGHT.*

Questions 1-10.

DIRECTIONS: Questions 1 through 10 are to be answered on the basis of the following information.

52 year-old Tim Brown visits his doctor after suffering for the last 3 days from pain in his legs and feet and numbness and tingling of the toes, and noticing shiny and taut skin with hair loss on his lower legs.

1. After being examined by the physician, Tim is diagnosed with arteriosclerosis obliterans. 1.___
The nurse, after being asked by Tim about the disease, explains to him that arteriosclerosis obliterans is a chronic occlusive _____ disease that may affect the _____.
   A. arterial; inferior vena cava or the extremities
   B. venous; superior vena cava or the extremities
   C. venous; pulmonary vessels or the extremities
   D. arterial; abdominal aorta or the lower extremities

2. The obstruction of blood flow with resultant ischemia usually does NOT affect the _____ artery. 2.___
   A. femoral
   B. aortal
   C. oesophageal
   D. iliac

3. Arteriosclerosis obliterans occurs MOST often in _____ ages _____. 3.___
   A. men; 40-50
   B. women; 40-50
   C. men; 50-60
   D. women; 50-60

4. Which of the following is NOT a risk factor for arteriosclerosis obliterans? 4.___
   A. Hypotension
   B. Cigarette smoking
   C. Hyperlipidemia
   D. Diabetes mellitus

5. While assessing Mr. Brown, the nurse expects to notice all of the following EXCEPT 5.___
   A. both intermittent claudication and rest pain
   B. pallor after 1-2 minutes of elevating feet
   C. diminished or absent radial pulse
   D. diminished or absent dorsalis pedis pulse

6. The one of the following that is NOT a diagnostic test for arteriosclerosis obliterans is 6.___
   A. oscillometry
   B. seriology
   C. angiography
   D. doppler ultrasound

7. Mr. Brown is tired of staying in his bed and wants to walk around. 7.___
   The nurse's BEST advice for him would be that he can
   A. not do any physical activity until he is completely recovered and discharged from the hospital
   B. leave his bed not more than once a day
   C. leave his bed twice a day but not leave the room
   D. leave his bed 3-4 times a day and walk twice a day

8. All of the following would be appropriate nursing interventions for Mr. Brown's recovery EXCEPT to 8.___
   A. assess for sensory function and trophic changes
   B. encourage slow, progressive physical activity
   C. order medications as required
   D. protect the patient from injury

9. Which of the following would NOT be appropriate teaching and discharge planning for the nurse to provide to Mr. Brown? 9.___
   The importance of
   A. a restricted kcal, high-saturated fat diet
   B. continuing with established exercise program
   C. avoiding constrictive clothing and standing in any position for a long time
   D. foot care, immediately taking care of cuts, wounds, and injuries

10. Doppler ultrasound is the most widely used method in arteriosclerosis obliterans. 10.___
    The SIMPLEST method for estimating blood flow to the lower extremities is to measure the _____ blood pressure at the level of the ankle and compare it to the _____ pressure.
    A. systolic; brachial diastolic
    B. diastolic; brachial diastolic
    C. systolic; brachial systolic
    D. systolic; femoral systolic

Questions 11-19.

DIRECTIONS: Questions 11 through 19 are to be answered on the basis of the following information.

32 year-old George Dawson visits the hospital after continuously experiencing coldness, tingling, numbness, and burning in all his extremities and, lately, getting an ulceration in one of his digits. Mr. Dawson is also a cigarette smoker.

11. After being examined by the physician, Mr. Dawson is diagnosed with thromboangiitis obliterans. Thromboangiitis obliterans is BEST defined as an 11.___
   A. acute, inflammatory disorder affecting small size arteries of the lower extremities
   B. obliterative disease characterized by inflammatory changes in medium sized veins of the lower extremities
   C. acute, inflammatory disorder affecting large sized arteries of the lower extremities
   D. obliterative disease characterized by inflammatory changes in small and medium sized arteries and veins

12. The symptoms and signs of thromboangiitis obliterans are those of arterial ischemia and of superficial phlebitis. A history of migratory phlebitis, usually in the veins of the foot or leg, is present in _____% of cases. 12.___
   A. 20 B. 30 C. 40 D. 50

13. Thromboangiitis obliterans occurs MOST often in _____ ages _____. 13.___
   A. men; 35-50 B. women; 35-50
   C. men; 25-40 D. women; 25-40

14. While assessing Mr. Dawson, the nurse expects to find all of the following EXCEPT 14.___
   A. intermittent claudication
   B. an increased posterior tibial pulse
   C. trophic changes
   D. ulceration and gangrene

15. _____ is NOT a diagnostic test for thromboangiitis obliterans. 15.___
   A. Angiography B. Contrast venography
   C. Oscillometry D. Doppler ultrasound

16. Which of the following would NOT be included among the appropriate nursing interventions to control Mr. Dawson's disease? 16.___
   A. Prepare the patient for surgery when required
   B. Provide vasodilators and analgesics as ordered
   C. Administer coagulants not more than once a day
   D. All of the above

17. All of the following are appropriate teaching and discharge information which should be provided by the nurse to Mr. Dawson EXCEPT the 17.___
   A. drug regimen, including names, dosages, frequency, and side effects
   B. need to avoid trauma to the affected extremity
   C. need to avoid heat and have a good airconditioner in the bedroom
   D. importance of stopping smoking

18. The only REALLY effective treatment for thromboangiitis obliterans is 18.___
    A. antibiotics
    B. corticosteroids
    C. anticoagulants
    D. cessation of smoking

19. In thromboangiitis obliterans, since the adventitia is usually more extensively infiltrated with fibroblasts, older lesions show periarterial fibrosis, which may involve the adjacent 19.___
    A. artery
    B. vein
    C. nerve
    D. all of the above

Questions 20-30.

DIRECTIONS: Questions 20 through 30 are to be answered on the basis of the following information.

30 year-old Sara Johnson got married six years ago. She never became pregnant, having used oral contraceptives. Now she visits the hospital after experiencing anxiety, fever, and chest pain.

20. After being examined by the physician, she is diagnosed with pulmonary embolism, which is BEST described as a(n) 20.___
    A. embolic obstruction to blood flow increasing venous pressure in the pulmonary artery and pulmonary hypotension
    B. embolic obstruction to blood flow involving the upper lobes of the lung because of higher blood flow
    C. lodgement of a blood clot in a pulmonary artery with subsequent obstruction of blood supply to the lung parenchyma
    D. lodgement of a blood clot in a pulmonary vein with subsequent obstruction of blood supply to the lung parenchyma

21. MOST pulmonary emboli arise as detached portions of venous thrombi formed in the 21.___
    A. deep veins of the legs
    B. right side of the heart
    C. pelvic area
    D. all of the above

22. Once released into the venous circulation, emboli are distributed to both lungs in about _____% of cases, to the right lung in _____% of cases, and to the left lung in _____% of cases. 22.___
    A. 45; 40; 30
    B. 55; 30; 20
    C. 65; 20; 10
    D. 75; 10; 5

23. _____ lobes are involved in pulmonary embolism _____ times more often than _____ lobes. 23.___
    A. lower; 2; upper
    B. upper; 2; lower
    C. lower; 4; upper
    D. upper; 4; lower

24. Which of the following is NOT a risk factor for Mrs. Johnson? 24.___
   A. Trauma
   B. Pregnancy
   C. Oral contraceptives
   D. Intrauterine contraceptive devices

25. While assessing Mrs. Johnson, the nurse expects to notice all of the following EXCEPT 25.___
   A. severe dyspnea and a feeling of impending doom
   B. tachypnea and bradycardia
   C. increased pH due to hyperventilation
   D. crackles due to intensified pulmonic S_2

26. Concerning the diagnosis of pulmonary embolism, it is NOT correct that 26.___
   A. pulmonary arteriography reveals location and/or extent of embolism
   B. lung scan reveals adequacy or inadequacy of pulmonary circulation
   C. clinical symptoms and signs should suggest the diagnosis
   D. none of the above

27. All of the following drugs would be used in drug therapy for Mrs. Johnson EXCEPT 27.___
   A. anticoagulants
   B. dextran 70 to decrease viscosity and aggregation of blood cells
   C. narcotics for pain relief
   D. vasodepressors in the presence of shock

28. The surgical procedure used for the correction of pulmonary embolism is known as 28.___
   A. pulmonary thrombolectomy
   B. cardiac embolectomy
   C. pulmonary embolectomy
   D. cardiac thrombolectomy

29. It would be appropriate for the nurse attending to Mrs. Johnson to do all of the following EXCEPT 29.___
   A. administer oxygen therapy to correct hypoxemia
   B. provide adequate hydration to prevent hypocoagulability
   C. elevate the head of the bed to relieve dyspnea
   D. assist with turning, coughing, deep breathing, and passive ROM exercises

30. Which of the following is NOT considered among the appropriate teaching and discharge planning provided by the nurse to Mrs. Johnson? 30.___
   A. Use of plastic stockings when ambulatory
   B. Need to avoid sitting or standing for long periods of time
   C. Drug regimen
   D. Gradually increase walking distance

KEY (CORRECT ANSWERS)

1. D
2. C
3. C
4. A
5. C

6. B
7. D
8. C
9. A
10. C

11. D
12. C
13. C
14. B
15. B

16. C
17. C
18. D
19. D
20. C

21. D
22. C
23. C
24. D
25. B

26. D
27. D
28. C
29. B
30. A

EXAMINATION SECTION

TEST 1

DIRECTIONS: Each question or incomplete statement is followed by several suggested answers or completions. Select the one that BEST answers the question or completes the statement. *PRINT THE LETTER OF THE CORRECT ANSWER IN THE SPACE AT THE RIGHT.*

1. Mothers of infants and toddlers should be instructed that diets for their children that include milk at the expense of other foods are MOST likely to result in the development of a deficiency in 1.___
   A. iron B. carbohydrate
   C. vitamin D D. vitamin K

2. A 1-week-old boy, weighing 6 pounds, has just been returned to the pediatric unit after having surgery for an intestinal obstruction. He has nasogastric suction and is receiving intravenous fluids via a venous cutdown. In addition to meeting the infant's special needs, which of these measures would be ESSENTIAL? 2.___
   A. Restraining all four of the baby's extremities
   B. Handling the baby as little as possible
   C. Explaining the equipment used in the baby's treatment to his mother so that she can assist the nurse with his care
   D. Spending time stroking the baby

3. A mother makes all of these comments about her infant daughter to the physician.
   Which one describes a characteristic MORE likely to be observed in an infant with hypothyroidism than in a normal 3-month-old infant? 3.___
   A. She smiles a lot.
   B. She's so good and she never cries.
   C. She notices her toys and she knows my voice.
   D. She seems to spend a great deal of time watching her hands.

Questions 4-7.

DIRECTIONS: Questions 4 through 7 are to be answered on the basis of the following information.

Bruce Alfonse, 9 years old, has an acute asthmatic attack and is admitted to the hospital because he did not respond to treatment in the emergency room. He has had bronchial asthma since early childhood.

4. Bruce is to receive 100 mg. of aminophylline intravenously.
   If the ampules of aminophylline available on Bruce's unit contain aminophylline gr. $7\frac{1}{2}$ in 10 cc. of solution, how much solution from the ampule will contain 100 mg. of aminophylline? 4.___
   A. 2 cc. B. 4 cc. C. 6 cc. D. 8 cc.

5. Which of these events in Bruce's life would be MOST likely to cause an increase in the frequency and intensity of his asthmatic attacks? 5.___
   A. Ms. Alfonse's buying new furniture for Bruce's bedroom
   B. The Alfonse's moving to another city
   C. Mr. Alfonse's being away from home on business for several days
   D. Bruce's favorite grandparent's coming to visit for a week

6. An IMPORTANT objective of the medical and nursing management of Bruce should be to help him to 6.___
   A. accept the fact that he cannot be like other children and that he will have to limit his goals
   B. accept his condition and live a productive life
   C. understand the underlying cause of his condition
   D. accept being dependent upon his mother until he is in his middle teens

7. The nurse is planning Bruce's care. 7.___
   Consideration should be given to the fact that most normal 8-year-olds
   A. prefer to associate with a peer of the same sex
   B. seek opportunities for socializing with older boys
   C. enjoy small heterosexual groups
   D. function best as a member of a large group of somewhat younger boys and girls

Questions 8-13.

DIRECTIONS: Questions 8 through 13 are to be answered on the basis of the following information.

Jeff Green, age $2\frac{1}{2}$, sustained a simple fracture of the shaft of the left femur when he fell down stairs at home. Upon his admission to the hospital, Jeff is placed in Bryant's traction.

8. Among the equipment used in the application of Bryant's traction is 8.___
   A. adhesive material on the skin of both limbs
   B. metal calipers in the malleoli of both ankles
   C. a Kirschner wire in the affected femur
   D. a Thomas splint on the fractured extremity

9. During his first two days in the hospital, Jeff lies quietly, sucks his thumb, and does not cry. 9.___
   It is MOST justifiable to say that he
   A. has made a good adjustment to the traction
   B. is accustomed to being disciplined at home
   C. has confidence in the nurses caring for him
   D. is experiencing anxiety

10. Prior to his admission, Jeff was partially bowel-trained, but now he defecates involuntarily. 10.___
The nurse's approach to this problem should be based on which of these assessments?
   A. What is Jeff's reaction to his soiling
   B. How compulsive is Jeff about cleanliness
   C. Is Jeff too young for bowel training
   D. Is bowel training important for Jeff

11. Ms. Green is upset because when she comes to visit, Jeff turns his head away from her and holds his arms out to the nurse. 11.___
It is probably MOST justifiable to say that Jeff
   A. is angry with his mother for leaving him in the hospital
   B. is testing the relationship between his mother and the nurse
   C. now has a stronger emotional tie with the nurse than with his mother
   D. is consciously trying to make his mother jealous

12. One day when the nurse offers Jeff a cookie, he says *No!* and at the same time holds out his hand for it. 12.___
Which of these interpretations of Jeff's behavior is PROBABLY justifiable?
   A. His mother has forbidden sweets, and he is in conflict about accepting any.
   B. He is confused about the meaning of yes and no.
   C. His negativism is a beginning attempt at independence.
   D. He is unaccustomed to being offered choices.

13. To prevent accidents such as Jeff's among toddlers, which one of the following measures would probably help MOST? 13.___
   A. Having carpeting on stairs
   B. Using adjustable gates on stairways
   C. Providing the toddler with a plentiful supply of play materials in one room
   D. Keeping the toddler in a playpen placed near the mother's work area

Questions 14-19.

DIRECTIONS: Questions 14 through 18 are to be answered on the basis of the following information.

Adam Crane, 13 years old, is admitted to the hospital for treatment of acute rheumatic fever. He is placed on bed rest.

14. Adam MOST probably has which of these groups of symptoms that are characteristic of acute rheumatic fever? 14.___
   A. Swelling of the fingers, petechiae, and general malaise
   B. Nodules overlying bony prominences, dependent edema, and elevated blood pressure
   C. Bleeding gums, dyspnea, and failure to gain weight
   D. Fever, rash, and migratory joint pain

15. Adam is receiving a corticosteroid drug. 15.___
He should be observed for common side effects of this type of drug therapy, such as
A. hypotension
B. weight loss
C. pallor
D. acne

16. An oral potassium preparation is ordered for Adam. 16.___
The CHIEF purpose of this drug for him is to
A. promote excretion of bacterial toxins
B. prevent hypokalemia
C. enhance the action of the corticosteroid drug
D. reduce the electrical potential of the cardiac conduction system

17. Adam's blood tests include all of the following results. 17.___
Which of these results would be MOST indicative of improvement in his condition?
A. Positive C-reactive protein
B. Hemoglobin, 14.0 Gm. per 100 cc. of blood
C. White blood cell count, 11,000 per cu. mm. of blood
D. Decreasing erythrocyte sedimentation rate

18. Permanent functional impairment would MOST likely result if Adam developed 18.___
A. erythema marginatum
B. polyarthritis
C. carditis
D. subcutaneous nodules

19. Recurrent attacks of rheumatic fever in Adam can BEST be prevented by 19.___
A. keeping him on prophylactic drug therapy for an indefinite period
B. including foods in his diet that are rich in vitamins and minerals
C. improving his family's socioeconomic condition
D. providing daily afternoon rest periods for him for about a year after recovery from an acute attack

Questions 20-25.

DIRECTIONS: Questions 20 through 25 are to be answered on the basis of the following information.

Daniel Rich, 6 weeks old, is admitted to the pediatric unit with pyloric stenosis. He is to have a pyloromyotomy.

20. Daniel's parents tell the nurse that they do not quite understand what the doctor has told them about the operation, and they ask for clarification. 20.___
Which of these explanations to the parents would be MOST appropriate?
A. Daniel's stomach is contracted and its capacity diminished, making it necessary for the doctor to dilate it with instruments.

B. Nerves have produced contraction of certain muscles in Daniel's stomach called sphincters, and these nerves must be cut in order to produce relaxation.
C. Constricting bands of tissue in the middle of Daniel's stomach, which are causing vomiting, will be resected.
D. The doctor will make a cut in a tight muscle at the bottom of Daniel's stomach, which has caused his symptoms.

21. Preoperatively, Daniel is to receive 0.15 mg. (gr. 1/400) of atropine sulfate. 21.___
If a vial containing 0.4 mg. (gr. 1/150) in 1 cc. of solution is used to prepare Daniel's dose, how much of the stock solution should be given to him?
_____ cc.
A. 0.28 B. 0.33 C. 0.38 D. 0.43

22. Daniel should be observed for early symptoms of side effects of atropine, which include 22.___
A. vomiting and subnormal temperature
B. lethargy and bradycardia
C. rapid respirations and flushed skin
D. muscle spasms and diaphoresis

23. Daniel has a pyloromyotomy. 23.___
Assuming that Daniel's operation is successful, his parents should be informed that his convalescence can be expected to be
A. *gradual*, with the persistence of mild preoperative symptoms for a few weeks
B. *prolonged*, with gradual reduction and eventual disappearance of preoperative symptoms over a period of a few months
C. *brief*, but with periodic recurrence of preoperative symptoms during his first 6 months of life
D. *rapid*, and characterized by the absence of preoperative symptoms

24. Daniel is now 8 weeks old. 24.___
He should be expected to
A. cry when a stranger approaches
B. pay attention to a voice
C. laugh aloud
D. make sounds such as *ba-ba* and *da-da*

25. In response to Ms. Rich's questions, the nurse discusses with her the introduction of new foods into Daniel's diet. 25.___
Which of these suggestions by the nurse would be MOST appropriate?
A. Whenever a new food is added to Daniel's diet, decrease the amount of milk offered to him.
B. Give Daniel new foods one at a time.
C. Allow Daniel to touch each new solid food before he tastes it.
D. Mix new foods with a small amount of some food Daniel has previously had.

KEY (CORRECT ANSWERS)

1. A
2. D
3. B
4. A
5. B

6. B
7. A
8. A
9. D
10. A

11. A
12. C
13. B
14. D
15. D

16. B
17. D
18. C
19. A
20. D

21. C
22. C
23. D
24. B
25. B

TEST 2

DIRECTIONS: Each question or incomplete statement is followed by several suggested answers or completions. Select the one that BEST answers the question or completes the statement. *PRINT THE LETTER OF THE CORRECT ANSWER IN THE SPACE AT THE RIGHT.*

1. Parents are given information relative to the nutrition of normal newborn infants. 1.___
   Which of the following statements is INACCURATE?
   A. Formulas made of modified cow's milk are well absorbed.
   B. A high protein intake assures a rapid growth rate.
   C. The total daily intake of nutrients is more important than the size or frequency of individual feedings.
   D. Infants born of well-nourished mothers are likely to have adequate stores of nutrients at birth.

2. A 3-year-old has nephrosis and marked ascites. 2.___
   In which position is she likely to be MOST comfortable?
   A. Semi-Fowler's B. Sims'
   C. Dorsal recumbent D. Prone

3. A 5-year-old with leukemia is to be discharged because his condition is in a state of remission. 3.___
   It will be MOST helpful to the child when he is at home if his parents understand that
   A. the child's condition is terminal, and it will be their responsibility to make him as happy as possible without making demands upon him
   B. they should guide their child, encouraging him and setting limits for him, so that he may develop to his full potential
   C. it will not be necessary for them to control their child's behavior because his condition makes him aware of his own limitations
   D. it will be important for them to develop a carefully planned schedule for the child that will conserve his strength

Questions 4-7.

DIRECTIONS: Questions 4 through 7 are to be answered on the basis of the following information.

Josh Greene, 9½ months old, is admitted to the hospital. He has a provisional diagnosis of intussusception.

4. Josh MOST probably has which of these symptoms that are characteristic manifestations of the onset of intussusception in an infant? 4.___
   A. Abdominal distention and coffee-ground vomitus
   B. Hyperpyrexia and rectal prolapse
   C. Passage of large amount of flatus associated with straining
   D. Paroxysmal abdominal pain accompanied by screaming

5. When the physician tells Mr. and Ms. Greene that immediate surgery will be necessary if Josh's diagnosis is confirmed, they are reluctant to give permission for the operation. If surgery is not performed soon after a diagnosis of intussusception is made, which of these conditions is LIKELY to result? 5.___
   A. Chronic ulcerative colitis
   B. Megacolon
   C. Meckel's diverticulum
   D. Gangrene of the bowel

6. A barium enema is ordered to help confirm Josh's diagnosis. An additional reason why a barium enema is ordered for Josh at this time is that it may result in 6.___
   A. elimination of offending toxins
   B. diminution of microbial flora of the intestine in preparation for surgery
   C. control of bleeding due to the barium's astringent effect on the bowel lining
   D. reduction of the telescoped bowel segment

7. Josh has intussusception, and the condition is corrected by surgery. His recovery is satisfactory. When Josh begins to feel better, the play material that would probably be MOST appropriate for him is a 7.___
   A. mobile
   B. beanbag
   C. roly-poly animal with a weighted base
   D. tinker toy with parts securely fastened

Questions 8-15.

DIRECTIONS: Questions 8 through 15 are to be answered on the basis of the following information.

Amy Simpson, 13½ years old, is in the hospital for treatment of newly diagnosed diabetes mellitus. A teaching program for Amy and her mother has been instituted by the nursing staff.

8. To plan a teaching program for Amy, the nurse should consider that the factor that will have the GREATEST influence on its success is 8.___
   A. the child's age
   B. the child's parents' acceptance of the diagnosis
   C. whether or not teaching is done consistently by the same nurse
   D. whether or not teaching is limited to one-hour periods

9. When teaching Amy and her parents about insulin, it is important to include the fact that insulin 9.___
   A. requirements will decrease with age
   B. dosage is determined, primarily, on the basis of daily food intake
   C. dosage, after adolescence, can be adjusted by the person in terms of variations in physical activity
   D. will be needed for life

10. One morning when the nurse goes to help Amy with morning care, Amy is argumentative and restless. She makes unkind remarks to the other children. 10.___
It is essential for the nurse to give IMMEDIATE consideration to which of these questions?
   A. Does Amy need a more structured plan of care?
   B. When did Amy have her insulin and did she eat her breakfast?
   C. Was there some incident that occurred the previous day that has upset Amy?
   D. Is Amy bored and does she need help in selecting recreational activities that will utilize her excess energy?

11. One day Amy asks the nurse, *Will I be able to go with the gang after school to get ice cream or a hot dog?* 11.___
Which of these responses by the nurse would give Amy accurate information?
   A. You can go with the group, but the hot dogs, ice cream, and other foods that they eat are prohibited for you. Your friends will learn to be considerate of your special needs.
   B. Both hot dogs and ice cream contain valuable nutrients. But if you have a hot dog, don't eat the roll.
   C. You can have a hot dog if you omit a corresponding amount of food from your next meal. Since sweets are not good for you, avoid foods like ice cream.
   D. Being with your friends is important. You can eat a hot dog or ice cream sometimes. We'll help you learn how to choose foods.

12. One day Amy tells her mother and the nurse that she does not want to give herself insulin. Her mother says to her, *You don't have to give yourself the injection if you don't want to. I'll do it for you.* 12.___
Which of these understandings should be the basis of the nurse's response?
   A. The mother must be helped to understand the importance of the girl's participation in her own care.
   B. The girl needs to assume responsibility for her treatment; therefore, Amy and her mother should be taught separately.
   C. Children with diabetes often rebel against puncturing themselves with needles, and teaching should be discontinued until signs of readiness are demonstrated.
   D. The reaction of the mother is normal and should be overlooked.

13. A few days before Amy is discharged, her scout leader visits her. The scout leader stops at the nurses' station before leaving and says, *The troop is going on a four-day camping trip next month. Amy is very eager to go, and I'd like to have her come. But I'm rather concerned about having her out in the woods with us.* 13.___
Before replying, which of these questions should the nurse consider?
   A. Are such trips contraindicated for children who have diabetes?
   B. Would it be too hazardous for Amy to attempt the trip so soon after her hospitalization?
   C. Will there be an adult accompanying the children who has had experience with children who have diabetes?
   D. Does Amy have enough information about her condition so that she is unlikely to have any difficulty?

14. Ms. Simpson says to the nurse, *Amy has never been a complainer. I'm afraid that she will not tell me if she doesn't feel well before she goes to school.* 14.___
Which of these responses by the nurse would be MOST helpful to Amy's mother?
   A. It will be important to find out how Amy is feeling without stressing symptoms in talking with her.
   B. It is the school nurse's responsibility to help you with problems like this.
   C. Since Amy behaves this way, it will be necessary for you to question her frequently about how she feels.
   D. You don't need to worry about this because when Amy leaves the hospital her diabetes will be controlled.

15. In the management of a child with diabetes mellitus, occasional minimal glycosuria may be allowed. 15.___
The purpose of this management is to
   A. retard degenerative tissue changes
   B. detect early symptoms of impending coma
   C. reduce the incidence of insulin shock
   D. facilitate diet supervision

Questions 16-22.

DIRECTIONS: Questions 16 through 22 are to be answered on the basis of the following information.

Jimmy Brown, 6 years old, is brought to the hospital immediately after sustaining burns that occurred in his home when he pulled a pan of boiling water off the stove. He has severe burns, mostly third degree, of the anterior chest, upper arms, forearms, and hands.

Jimmy is placed in a single room. An intravenous infusion is started, an indwelling urethral (Foley) catheter is inserted, and pressure dressings are applied to his burned areas.

16. Jimmy develops burn shock. He can be expected to exhibit 16.___
   A. restlessness and bradycardia
   B. air hunger and hyperreflexia
   C. intense pain and convulsions
   D. pale, clammy skin and thirst

17. To plan for Jimmy's fluid replacement needs, it should be noted that the 17.___
   A. younger the child, the greater amount of fluid he needs in proportion to his body weight
   B. proportion of body weight contributed by water is smaller during early childhood than it is during adulthood
   C. fluid needs per kilogram of body weight are variable until the kidneys become functionally mature at adolescence
   D. total volume of extracellular fluid per kilogram of body weight increases gradually from birth to adolescence and then stabilizes at the adult level

18. On admission, Jimmy's rectal temperature was 99°F. (37.2°C.) Twelve hours later, it is 101.6°F. (38.7°C.). On the basis of the information provided about him, it is MOST justified to say that it 18.___
   A. is an expected development in injuries such as Jimmy's
   B. is indicative of damage to Jimmy's heat-control center
   C. is a manifestation of rapidly spreading infection
   D. has resulted chiefly from a marked increase in serum potassium

19. Twenty-four hours after his admission, Jimmy complains that his chest dressing feels too tight. The nurse should FIRST 19.___
   A. check Jimmy's respirations
   B. loosen the chest bandage
   C. call the doctor
   D. find out whether Jimmy has a p.r.n. order for an analgesic

20. When selecting a site for the administration of a parenteral drug to Jimmy, it would be MOST important for the nurse to consider that 20.___
   A. impaired circulation hampers drug absorption
   B. decreased blood volume shortens the period of drug action
   C. drug action is potentiated by increased amounts of circulating epinephrine
   D. concentration of blood plasma in the tissues potentiates the desired effects of drugs

21. Which of these meals for Jimmy would be HIGHEST in proteins and calories? 21.___
   A. Vegetable soup, cottage cheese on crackers, applesauce, hot chocolate
   B. Cheeseburger, french fried potatoes, carrot sticks, cantaloupe balls, milk
   C. Fresh fruit plate with sherbet, buttered muffin, slice of watermelon, fruit-flavored milk drink
   D. Chicken noodle soup, cream cheese and jelly sandwich, buttered whole kernel corn, orange sherbet, cola drink

22. Jimmy is scheduled to go to the physical therapy department at 9:30 A.M. every day. One morning at 8:30, after Jimmy has had his breakfast, the nurse who goes in to bathe him finds him sound asleep. 22.___
Which of these actions by the nurse would demonstrate the BEST judgment?
   A. Allow Jimmy to sleep until necessary equipment for his bath is gathered and then wake him for the procedure.
   B. Let Jimmy sleep and postpone his bath until sometime later in the day.
   C. Wake Jimmy gently and bathe him, explaining to him that he can rest when he returns from physical therapy
   D. Bathe Jimmy as quickly as possible and then let him sleep until it is time to go for physical therapy.

Questions 23-24.

DIRECTIONS: Questions 23 through 24 are to be answered on the basis of the following information.

Ralph Dunn, 15 years old, is admitted to the hospital for treatment of ulcerative colitis.

23. Ralph is receiving methantheline (Banthine) bromide. The CHIEF purpose of this drug for Ralph is to 23.___
   A. suppress inflammation of the bowel
   B. reduce peristaltic activity
   C. neutralize acid in the gastrointestinal tract
   D. increase bowel tone

24. Ralph is on a low-residue, high-protein, high-calorie diet. 24.___
To meet the requirements of Ralph's diet prescription, the nurse should guide Ralph to select as an evening snack
   A. a roast beef sandwich
   B. strawberry shortcake with whipped cream
   C. canned peaches
   D. fresh orange juice

25. The nurse is discussing nutrition with the mother of two sons, a preadolescent and an adolescent. 25.___
The mother should be instructed that in terms of nutritional needs, as compared with most normal preadolescent boys, MOST normal adolescent boys need _____ calories _____ protein.
A. more; but less
B. more; and more
C. fewer; but more
D. fewer; and less

KEY (CORRECT ANSWERS)

1. B
2. A
3. B
4. D
5. D

6. D
7. C
8. B
9. D
10. B

11. D
12. A
13. C
14. A
15. C

16. D
17. A
18. A
19. A
20. A

21. B
22. B
23. B
24. A
25. B

EXAMINATION SECTION

TEST 1

DIRECTIONS: Each question or incomplete statement is followed by several suggested answers or completions. Select the one that BEST answers the question or completes the statement. *PRINT THE LETTER OF THE CORRECT ANSWER IN THE SPACE AT THE RIGHT.*

1. Which of these occurrences in a postpartal woman would be MOST indicative of an abnormality? 1.___
   A. A chill shortly after delivery
   B. A pulse rate of 60 the morning after delivery
   C. Urinary output of 3,000 ml. on the second day after delivery
   D. An oral temperature of 101°F. (38.3°C.) on the third day after delivery

2. While discussing nutrition with the nurse, a woman who is a primigravida says that she eats an egg for breakfast every day. 2.___
   The woman should be informed that the absorption of iron from the egg would be BEST facilitated by the woman's also eating _____ at the same meal.
   A. toast
   B. butter
   C. orange juice
   D. bacon

Questions 3-8.

DIRECTIONS: Questions 3 through 8 are to be answered on the basis of the following information.

Ms. Judy Lee, 28 years old and gravida I, is attending the antepartal clinic regularly. Ms. Lee is carrying twins. In the 38th week of gestation, she is admitted to the hospital in labor. Her membranes have ruptured.

3. Since Ms. Lee's admission, the nurse has been able to hear and count the heartbeats of both twins. Suppose that at a later time during Ms. Lee's labor, the nurse can hear only one heartbeat, even after several attempts. Which of these interpretations of this finding would be ACCURATE? 3.___
   A. Inaudibility of one of the heartbeats can result from a change in the position of the twins, but it could also be due to fetal distress; prompt evaluation of the situation by the physician is mandatory.
   B. Muffled fetal heartbeats are common when uterine contractions are strong and frequent, as they are in a multiple pregnancy; more frequent evaluation of the fetal heartbeats is advisable.

C. Inability to hear one heartbeat in a twin pregnancy can normally be expected at intervals throughout labor; no action is indicated.
D. Inability to hear fetal heartbeats in a twin pregnancy does not indicate fetal difficulty unless accompanied by additional symptoms; amniotic fluid should be examined for meconium staining.

4. Ms. Lee's labor progresses, and she delivers spontaneously two girls - one weighs 4 lbs. (1,814 gm.) and the other weighs 4 lb. 8 oz. (2,041 gm.). The twins are transferred to the premature nursery, and Ms. Lee is transferred to the postpartum unit. 4.___
Which of these concepts should be MOST basic to planning care for the Lee twins?
A. Circulatory function is enhanced by frequent change of position.
B. A well-lubricated skin is resistant to excoriation and damage.
C. A premature infant's rectal temperature reflects the infant's ability to conserve heat.
D. Optimal environmental temperature results in minimal oxygen consumption in the premature infant.

5. The method used for a premature infant's first formula feeding and the time at which it is begun will be based CHIEFLY upon the infant's 5.___
A. birth weight
B. degree of hydration
C. level of physiologic maturity
D. total body surface

6. The smaller of the Lee twins is to be gavaged. 6.___
In determining the location of the catheter after its insertion into the infant, it would be MOST desirable to insert
A. the tip of a large syringe into the catheter and withdraw an amount of air equal to the amount of feeding
B. a few drops of sterile water into the catheter, hold the end of the catheter below the level of the infant's stomach, and observe it for drainage of gastric contents
C. about 0.5 to 1 ml. of air into the catheter and listen to the infant's abdomen with a stethoscope
D. about 5 ml. of sterile water into the catheter and observe the infant's respirations

7. On her second postpartum day, Ms. Lee says to the nurse, *I've been to the bathroom four times in the past hour to urinate. The funny thing about it is that I only pass a small amount of urine each time.* 7.___
Which of these initial actions by the nurse would demonstrate the BEST judgment?
A. Palpate Ms. Lee's abdomen for bladder distention.
B. Explain to Ms. Lee that frequent voiding is expected during the first few days after delivery.

C. Advise Ms. Lee to use a bedpan for her next voiding.
D. Discuss with Ms. Lee the relationship between trauma during delivery and signs of bladder irritation during the postpartum period.

8. On the third postpartum day, Ms. Lee is discharged. The twins are to remain until they have reached an appropriate weight. When the twins are to be discharged, Mr. and Ms. Lee come to the hospital to take them home. Which of these statements, if made by Ms. Lee, would indicate the BEST understanding of her babies' needs? 8.___
A. Our babies' needs are different from those of full-term infants, and we will do all we can to protect them.
B. We are going to try very hard to counteract the effects of our babies' having been born prematurely.
C. For a while the smaller baby will need special attention, and then we will be able to treat both of our babies similarly.
D. We expect to enjoy our babies and will give them the kind of care babies need.

Questions 9-18.

DIRECTIONS: Questions 9 through 18 are to be answered on the basis of the following information.

Ms. Angela Dobbs, 32 years old and gravida I, is now in her third trimester of pregnancy. She has had diabetes mellitus since the age of 16 and has been attending the antepartal clinic regularly for the past 5 months.

9. Compared with Ms. Dobbs' insulin requirements when she was not pregnant, it can be expected that the insulin dosage during her third trimester will 9.___
A. remain the same
B. be increased
C. be decreased
D. be increased or decreased, depending upon fetal activity

10. At 30 weeks' gestation, Ms. Dobbs has an ultrasonic examination. The results of this examination disclose information about the fetus' 10.___
A. circulatory function
B. gestational age
C. presence of surfactant
D. presence of congenital defects

11. Because the incidence of fetal death is higher in women who have diabetes mellitus, indications of placental insufficiency should be suspected if Ms. Dobbs has a(n) 11.___
A. sustained drop in her blood glucose level
B. urinary output of more than 1500 ml. a day
C. increase in the secretion of gonadotropin
D. albumin content in her urine of +1

12. At 35 weeks' gestation, Ms. Dobbs is admitted to the hospital for evaluation of her pregnancy and diabetic status. Ms. Dobbs is to have a urinary estriol level determination. 12.___
Which of these instructions should be among those given to her about collecting the urine for this procedure? Collect
   A. the first morning specimen before eating breakfast
   B. a specimen about an hour after the evening meal
   C. a twenty-four hour specimen
   D. a clean-voided specimen

13. Ms. Dobbs is to have an amniocentesis done to determine the lecithin/sphingomyelin (L/S) ratio. 13.___
The purpose of this study is to
   A. assess placental functioning
   B. assess the amount of fetal body fat
   C. determine fetal kidney functioning
   D. determine fetal pulmonary maturity

14. Ms. Dobbs has a cesarean section and is delivered of a boy who weighs 8 lb. 4 oz. (3,742 gm.). He is transferred to the intensive care nursery. Ms. Dobbs is transferred to the postpartum unit from the recovery room. 14.___
Postpartum orders for Ms. Dobbs include an estrogen preparation to
   A. promote sodium excretion
   B. suppress the production of chorionic gonadotropin
   C. inhibit secretion of the lactogenic hormone
   D. diminish lochial flow

15. Two hours after delivery, the nurse observes that Baby Boy Dobbs is lethargic and has developed mild generalized cyanosis and twitching. 15.___
In view of the fact that his mother has diabetes mellitus, the infant is PROBABLY exhibiting symptoms of a
   A. low blood sugar level   B. high CO_2 level
   C. subnormal temperature   D. withdrawal from insulin

16. Because Ms. Dobbs has diabetes mellitus, her infant should be assessed for the presence of 16.___
   A. a blood group incompatibility
   B. meconium ileus
   C. phenylketonuria
   D. a congenital abnormality

17. Ms. Dobbs is bottle-feeding her baby. Ms. Dobbs, who has previously observed a demonstration of diapering, is changing her baby's diaper for the first time, under the supervision of the registered nurse. Ms. Dobbs is holding the baby's feet correctly, but when she starts to raise his legs to remove the diaper, the feet slip from her grasp, and the baby's legs drop back onto the mattress of the bassinet. The baby whimpers briefly, and Ms. Dobbs looks dismayed. 17.___

Which of these responses by the nurse would be BEST?
A. I'll show you again how to change the baby's diaper, Ms. Dobbs.
B. I'll diaper the baby for you this time, Ms. Dobbs.
C. You've almost got it, Ms. Dobbs. Try again?
D. Why are you so nervous, Ms. Dobbs?

18. Some time after discharge, Ms. Dobbs calls the hospital to report the loss of her baby's birth certificate. Where would it be BEST for her to apply for a duplicate? The 18.___
A. record room of the hospital where the baby was born
B. agency that records vital statistics for the community in which the baby was born
C. Census Bureau
D. National Office of Vital Statistics

Questions 19-25.

DIRECTIONS: Questions 19 through 25 are to be answered on the basis of the following information.

Ms. Linda Young, a 17-year-old high school student, attends the antepartal clinic on a regular basis. This is Linda's first pregnancy.

19. Linda is now 7 months pregnant. In assessing whether Linda is retaining abnormal amounts of fluid, it would be ESPECIALLY significant that she has gained 19.___
A. 3 lb. (1,361 gm.) during the past week
B. 4½ lb. (2,041 gm.) since her last clinic visit a month ago
C. 11 lb. (4,990 gm.) in the second trimester of pregnancy
D. 14 lb. (6,350 gm.) since the onset of pregnancy

20. Which of these measures will contribute MOST to the prevention of postpartal uterine infections? 20.___
A. Routine use of serologic tests for syphilis early in the antepartal period
B. Limitation of sexual intercourse during the last six weeks of pregnancy
C. Maintenance of cleanliness of the perineal area during labor
D. Taking showers or sponge baths exclusively during the last six weeks of pregnancy

21. At term, Linda is admitted to the hospital in active labor. Linda's cervix is 2 cm. dilated and 80% effaced. Which of these interpretations of these findings is CORRECT? The 21.___
A. cervix is 2 cm. short of complete dilatation, and it is 80% thinner than it was before labor started

B. cervix is still 2 cm. long, and 80% of the thinning of the cervix is completed
C. walls of the cervix are 2 cm. thick, and 80% of the widening of the cervical opening has been achieved
D. opening of the cervix is 2 cm. wide, and the cervical canal is 80% shorter than normal

22. Linda has an episiotomy and delivers a 7 lb. (3,175 gm.) boy. Baby Boy Young is transferred to the nursery and Linda is transferred to the postpartum unit. Linda plans to bottle-feed her baby. The nurse is assessing Baby Boy Young. 22.___
Which of these observations, if made, would be considered characteristics of a newborn?
A. Branlike desquamation of the hands and fee; alternating limpness and stiffness of the body; and pink, moist skin
B. Cool, mottled hands and feet; quivering lower jaw; and flexion of body parts
C. Clenched fists; arching of the back when recumbent; and frequent crying
D. Butterfly-shaped area of pigmentation at the base of the spine; extension of the arms and legs when the head is turned to the side; and diaphragmatic breathing

23. When Linda has been admitted to the postpartum unit, she says to the nurse, *I'm so glad my baby is a boy. Maybe Jack will marry me now because he'll be so proud to have a son.* 23.___
It is probably MOST justifiable to say that Linda
A. wants to get married in order to gain her independence from her family
B. is capable of subordinating her personal needs to the needs of others
C. is showing a beginning awareness of the problems associated with having a baby out of wedlock
D. lacks insight into the factors that contribute to a successful marriage

24. When Baby Boy Young is brought to his mother for the first time to be fed, Linda asks the nurse, *What's wrong with my baby's eyes? He looks cross-eyed.* 24.___
Which of these initial responses by the nurse would probably be MOST helpful?
A. Babies seem to be cross-eyed for a while after birth because the muscles in their eyes aren't able to work together.
B. You feel that your baby's eyes are abnormal?
C. I can see that you're upset about this. It would be advisable for you to talk with the doctor about it.
D. Your baby will appear cross-eyed for some time because his eyes won't be completely developed until he is about six months old.

25. When Linda is talking with the nurse about feeding her baby, she says, *I've heard that if I breastfed him, he'd develop a close feeling toward me more quickly. I had planned to bottle-feed him.* 25.___
The nurse's initial reply should convey which of these understandings about the development of a mother-child relationship?
   A. A satisfactory mother-child relationship will develop more readily through breastfeeding than bottle-feeding.
   B. Holding the baby during bottle-feeding will help to promote a good mother-child relationship.
   C. The times at which the baby is fed by the mother will affect the quality of the mother-child relationship more than the feeding method.
   D. Since bottle-feeding is less complicated than breastfeeding, the mother will be able to focus more attention on mothering functions such as cuddling and talking while the baby is eating.

KEY (CORRECT ANSWERS)

1. D
2. C
3. A
4. D
5. C

6. C
7. A
8. D
9. B
10. B

11. A
12. C
13. D
14. C
15. A

16. D
17. C
18. B
19. A
20. C

21. D
22. B
23. D
24. A
25. B

TEST 2

DIRECTIONS: Each question or incomplete statement is followed by several suggested answers or completions. Select the one that BEST answers the question or completes the statement. *PRINT THE LETTER OF THE CORRECT ANSWER IN THE SPACE AT THE RIGHT.*

1. The instructions that are ESPECIALLY important to give to a pregnant woman who has heart disease are: 1.___
   A. Increase protein intake
   B. Take no drugs unless they have been prescribed
   C. Limit high-calorie foods
   D. Avoid fatigue

Questions 2-9.

DIRECTIONS: Questions 2 through 9 are to be answered on the basis of the following information.

Ms. Mary White, 35 years old, is pregnant for the third time. She is receiving antepartal care from a private physician. Ms. White is in the seventh month of pregnancy and has symptoms of preeclampsia.

2. The physician instructs Ms. White not to eat foods which have a high sodium content. The nurse tells Ms. White about foods containing sodium and then asks her to identify foods lowest in sodium. 2.___
   Which of these foods, if selected by Ms. White, would be CORRECT?
   A. Creamed chipped beef on dry toast
   B. Cheese sandwich on whole wheat toast
   C. Frankfurter on a roll
   D. Tomato stuffed with diced chicken

3. In Ms. White's 39th week of gestation, her physician recommends that she be hospitalized. When the physician leaves after examining Ms. White, Ms. White says to the nurse, *It's easy for you people to say, "Go to the hospital," but it's not so easy for me to do it. I can't go just like that!* 3.___
   After acknowledging her feeling, which of these approaches by the nurse would probably be BEST?
   A. Stress to Ms. White that her husband would want her to do what is best for her health.
   B. Explore with Ms. White ways that immediate hospitalization could be arranged.
   C. Repeat the physician's reasons for advising immediate hospitalization for Ms. White.
   D. Explain to Ms. White that she is ultimately responsible for her own welfare and that of her baby.

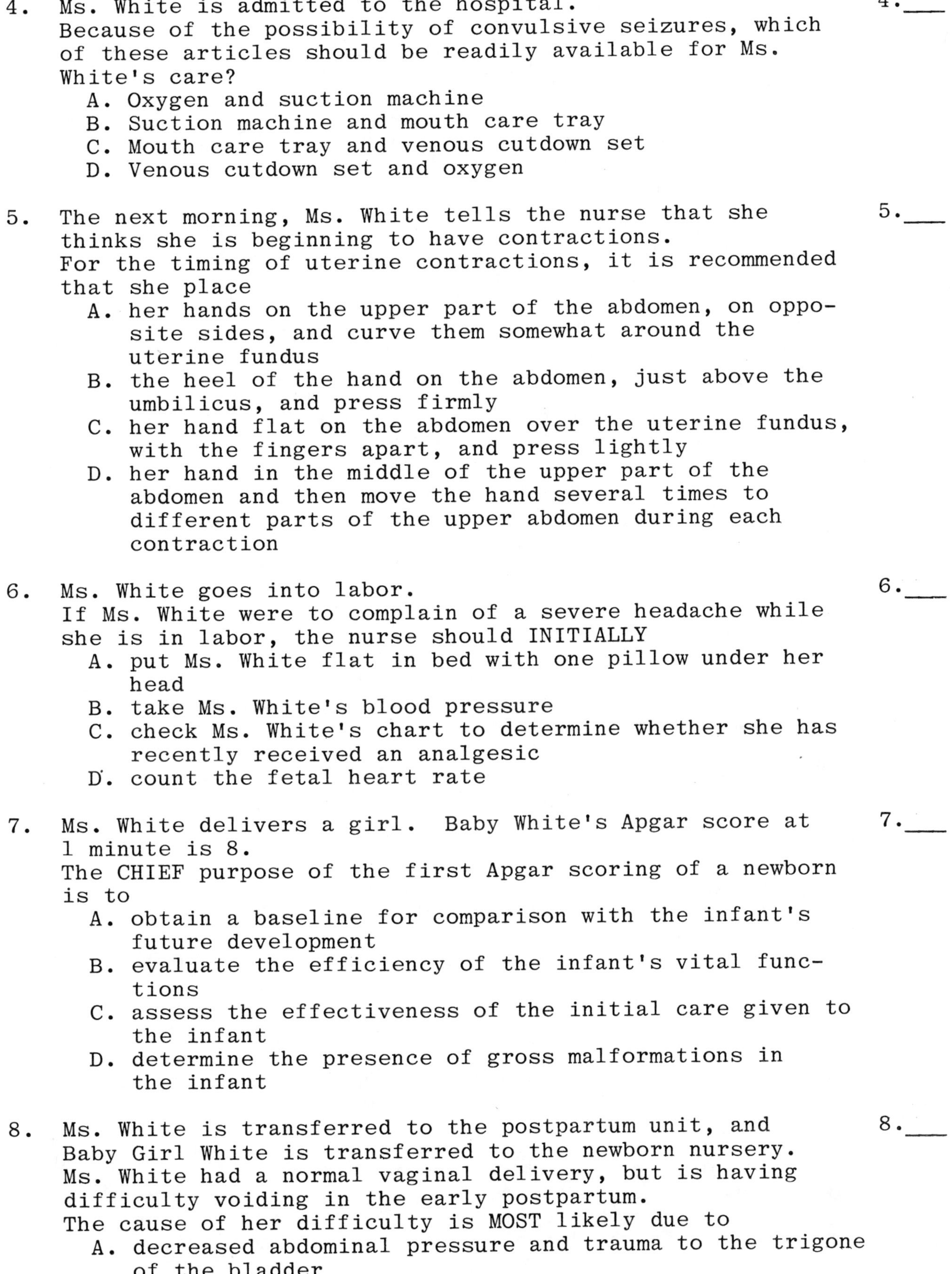

4. Ms. White is admitted to the hospital. 4.___
Because of the possibility of convulsive seizures, which of these articles should be readily available for Ms. White's care?
   A. Oxygen and suction machine
   B. Suction machine and mouth care tray
   C. Mouth care tray and venous cutdown set
   D. Venous cutdown set and oxygen

5. The next morning, Ms. White tells the nurse that she thinks she is beginning to have contractions. 5.___
For the timing of uterine contractions, it is recommended that she place
   A. her hands on the upper part of the abdomen, on opposite sides, and curve them somewhat around the uterine fundus
   B. the heel of the hand on the abdomen, just above the umbilicus, and press firmly
   C. her hand flat on the abdomen over the uterine fundus, with the fingers apart, and press lightly
   D. her hand in the middle of the upper part of the abdomen and then move the hand several times to different parts of the upper abdomen during each contraction

6. Ms. White goes into labor. 6.___
If Ms. White were to complain of a severe headache while she is in labor, the nurse should INITIALLY
   A. put Ms. White flat in bed with one pillow under her head
   B. take Ms. White's blood pressure
   C. check Ms. White's chart to determine whether she has recently received an analgesic
   D. count the fetal heart rate

7. Ms. White delivers a girl. Baby White's Apgar score at 1 minute is 8. 7.___
The CHIEF purpose of the first Apgar scoring of a newborn is to
   A. obtain a baseline for comparison with the infant's future development
   B. evaluate the efficiency of the infant's vital functions
   C. assess the effectiveness of the initial care given to the infant
   D. determine the presence of gross malformations in the infant

8. Ms. White is transferred to the postpartum unit, and Baby Girl White is transferred to the newborn nursery. 8.___
Ms. White had a normal vaginal delivery, but is having difficulty voiding in the early postpartum.
The cause of her difficulty is MOST likely due to
   A. decreased abdominal pressure and trauma to the trigone of the bladder

B. decreased blood volume and increased production of estrogen and progesterone
C. increased bladder tone and emotional stress
D. constriction of the kidney pelves and ureters

9. Ms. White is bottle-feeding her baby. Which of these manifestations developing in her nipples or breasts on the third day after delivery would be NORMAL? 9.___
A. Decrease in secretion from the breasts
B. Engorgement of the breasts
C. Inversion of the nipples
D. Tenderness and redness of the nipples

Questions 10-11.

DIRECTIONS: Questions 10 and 11 are to be answered on the basis of the following information.

Ms. Ellen Stone, an 18-year-old primigravida, is brought to the hospital in early active labor. She has received no antepartal care during her pregnancy.

10. Which of these observations of Ms. Stone would be the MOST reliable indication that she is in true labor? 10.___
A. Strong, intermittent uterine contractions
B. Progressive cervical effacement and dilatation
C. Rupture of the membranes
D. Engagement of the presenting part

11. During the first stage of Ms. Stone's labor, which of these measures by the nurse would be MOST supportive of her? 11.___
A. Administering sufficient analgesia to minimize pain from uterine contractions and encouraging her to remain on her back
B. Keeping her informed about the progress of her labor and helping her to relax between contractions
C. Having her hold on to the nurse's hand during the height of contractions and reminding her to breathe rapidly with her mouth open
D. Telling her to bear down with her contractions and instructing her to sleep between contractions

Questions 12-21.

DIRECTIONS: Questions 12 through 21 are to be answered on the basis of the following information.

Ms. Karen Newman, a 26-year-old multipara, is pregnant. Her obstetric history includes 2 full-term pregnancies terminating in normal deliveries and, prior to her present pregnancy, a spontaneous abortion at 14 weeks' gestation. She is receiving antepartal care from a private physician.

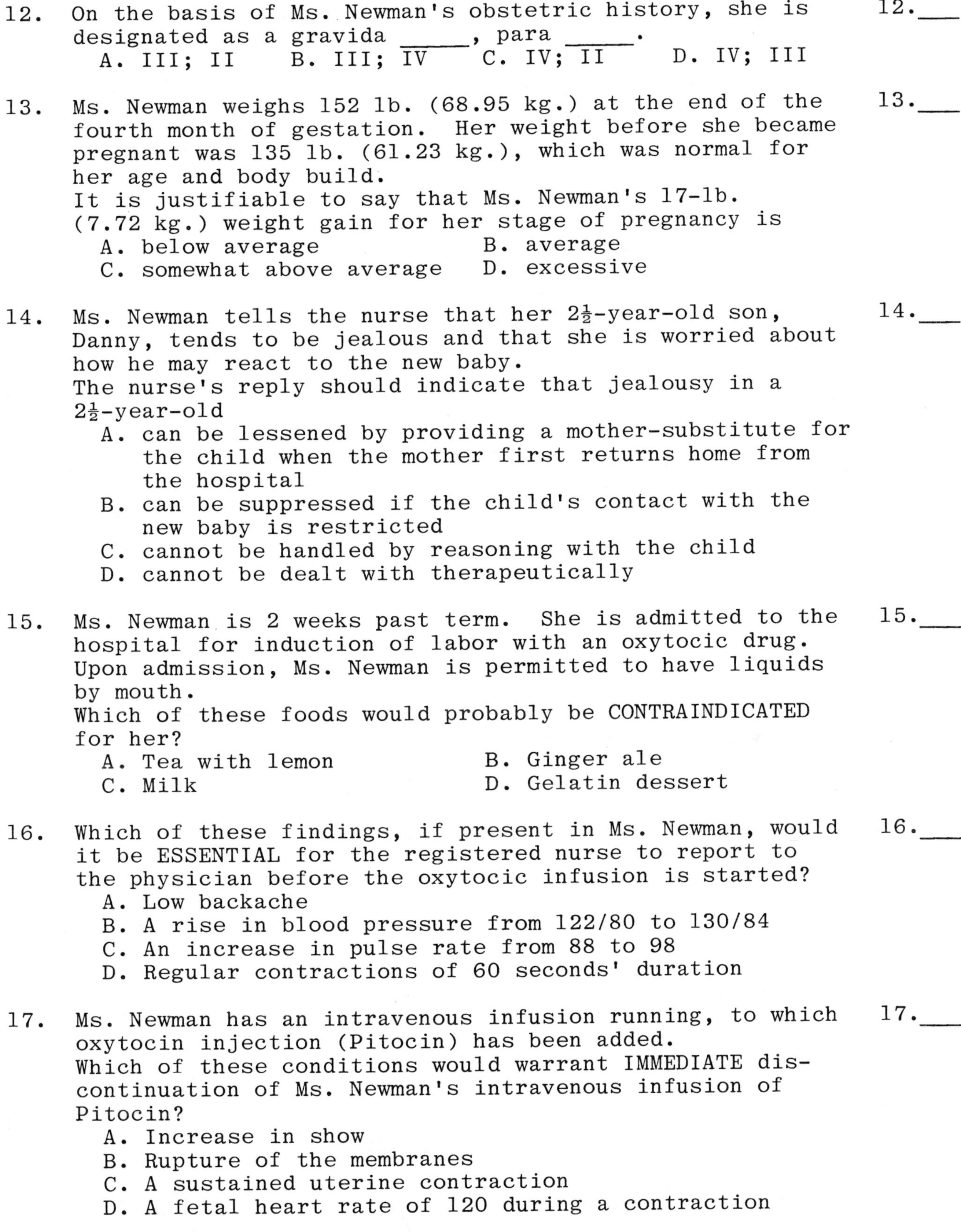

12. On the basis of Ms. Newman's obstetric history, she is designated as a gravida _____, para _____. 12.___
   A. III; II B. III; IV C. IV; II D. IV; III

13. Ms. Newman weighs 152 lb. (68.95 kg.) at the end of the fourth month of gestation. Her weight before she became pregnant was 135 lb. (61.23 kg.), which was normal for her age and body build. 13.___
It is justifiable to say that Ms. Newman's 17-lb. (7.72 kg.) weight gain for her stage of pregnancy is
   A. below average B. average
   C. somewhat above average D. excessive

14. Ms. Newman tells the nurse that her $2\frac{1}{2}$-year-old son, Danny, tends to be jealous and that she is worried about how he may react to the new baby. 14.___
The nurse's reply should indicate that jealousy in a $2\frac{1}{2}$-year-old
   A. can be lessened by providing a mother-substitute for the child when the mother first returns home from the hospital
   B. can be suppressed if the child's contact with the new baby is restricted
   C. cannot be handled by reasoning with the child
   D. cannot be dealt with therapeutically

15. Ms. Newman is 2 weeks past term. She is admitted to the hospital for induction of labor with an oxytocic drug. Upon admission, Ms. Newman is permitted to have liquids by mouth. 15.___
Which of these foods would probably be CONTRAINDICATED for her?
   A. Tea with lemon B. Ginger ale
   C. Milk D. Gelatin dessert

16. Which of these findings, if present in Ms. Newman, would it be ESSENTIAL for the registered nurse to report to the physician before the oxytocic infusion is started? 16.___
   A. Low backache
   B. A rise in blood pressure from 122/80 to 130/84
   C. An increase in pulse rate from 88 to 98
   D. Regular contractions of 60 seconds' duration

17. Ms. Newman has an intravenous infusion running, to which oxytocin injection (Pitocin) has been added. 17.___
Which of these conditions would warrant IMMEDIATE discontinuation of Ms. Newman's intravenous infusion of Pitocin?
   A. Increase in show
   B. Rupture of the membranes
   C. A sustained uterine contraction
   D. A fetal heart rate of 120 during a contraction

18. Ms. Newman has an order for 100 mg. of meperidine (Demerol) hydrochloride. 18.___
Which of these groups of signs in Ms. Newman would MOST clearly indicate that a dose of Demerol could be given to her with safety?
Cervical dilatation, _____ cm.; presenting part at _____ station; uterine contractions q. _____ minutes, lasting _____ seconds; fetal heart rate, _____ beats per minute.
A. 3; 0; 10; 45; 100
B. 4; 0; 3; 50; 172
C. 5; -1; 5; 40; 144
D. 7; -1; 2; 60; 120

19. In view of the fact that Ms. Newman had general anesthesia, it would be safe to start giving her oral fluids 19.___
A. after she voids for the first time
B. after she has coughed voluntarily
C. when her pulse rate is 70 beats per minute
D. when she has rested for about an hour after admission to the postpartum unit

20. Penicillin ointment rather than silver nitrate is used in the prophylactic eye care of Baby Boy Newman to 20.___
A. promote a more lasting bacteriostatic effect
B. gain a more rapid systemic effect
C. administer therapeutic amounts with greater ease
D. cause less irritation of the conjunctivae

21. Six weeks after the birth of her baby, Ms. Newman returns to the clinic for a routine follow-up visit. At the clinic, Ms. Newman says to the nurse, *Having so many children makes it very hard for us to manage, but my husband won't do anything to prevent me from getting pregnant. He gets angry when I even mention the idea.* 21.___
Which of these approaches by the nurse is LIKELY to be MOST useful?
A. Give Ms. Newman a pamphlet for her husband that describes various contraceptive methods.
B. Ask Ms. Newman to have her husband accompany her to the clinic to talk with the nurse about contraception.
C. Refer Ms. Newman to an agency that provides family planning services.
D. Find out from Ms. Newman if her husband would be willing to accept a method of contraception that would not involve him directly.

Questions 22-30.

DIRECTIONS: Questions 22 through 30 are to be answered on the basis of the following information.

Ms. Barbara Wing, 21 years old, attends the antepartal clinic for the first time when she has missed two menstrual periods. The physician determines that she is pregnant and finds her to be in good health. This is her first pregnancy.

22. During Ms. Wing's initial conference with the registered nurse, she mentions that although she usually feels well, there are times when she feels tired. 22.___
Which of these responses by the nurse would be BEST?
   A. Fatigue is normal when the body is adjusting to the pregnant state. Let's talk about your daily schedule so we can plan extra rest for you.
   B. It will be necessary for you to cut down on your usual activities and try to get more rest. About how many hours of sleep do you get at night?
   C. Your fatigue is probably due to hormonal changes that occur in early pregnancy. As your body adapts to the demands of your developing baby, this feeling will pass.
   D. Your fatigue at this time indicates that you probably will have to give special consideration to rest, and possibly even to diet, throughout your pregnancy.

23. Ms. Wing is to include extra amounts of vitamin C in her diet. 23.___
She should be instructed that the juice that has the LEAST vitamin C per average serving is
   A. canned apple
   B. canned tomato
   C. fresh grapefruit
   D. frozen orange

24. Ms. Wing's pregnancy progresses normally. 24.___
In the latter part of the third trimester, Ms. Wing should be advised to take which of these precautions relative to bathing?
   A. Take sponge baths exclusively
   B. Avoid using bath salts
   C. Bathe only in tepid water
   D. Place nonskid material at the bottom of the bathtub

25. Ms. Wing is at term and in early active labor when she is brought to the hospital by her husband. Mr. and Ms. Wing attended a series of preparation for childbirth classes. 25.___
Such a program is MOST likely to be successful if the
   A. parents and the medical and nursing staff have accepted the philosophy, principles, and techniques of the classes
   B. physician is present during labor and gives support to the mother
   C. nurse who is to stay with the mother during labor and delivery is prepared to assist the father in coaching his wife
   D. mother and father are truly prepared for their roles during labor and delivery

26. The nurse makes all of the following observations of Ms. Wing during the second stage of her labor. 26.___
Which one would be of GREATEST significance in terms of her welfare and that of her baby?
A(n)
   A. sudden increase in blood-tinged show
   B. change in the baseline blood pressure from 110/80 to 90/60

C. fetal heart rate of 152 to 160 beats per minute between contractions
D. increase in maternal pulse rate from 90 to 95 beats per minute during contractions

27. Ms. Wing has an episiotomy and delivers a girl weighing 7 lb. 5 oz. (3,317 gm.). 27.___
Which of these observations of Ms. Wing would indicate that normal placental separation is occurring?
She has
A. hardening and thickening of the exposed portion of the umbilical cord, softening of the uterine fundus, and a steady stream of blood from the vagina
B. strong uterine contractions, recession of the uterine fundus below the symphysis pubis, and temporary absence of vaginal bleeding
C. gaping of the vulva in conjunction with strong uterine contractions, rapid enlargement of the uterus, and oozing of blood from the vagina
D. increased protrusion of the umbilical cord from the vagina, the uterus' becoming globular-shaped, and a sudden spurting of blood from the vagina

28. Ms. Wing is transferred to the postpartum unit, and Baby Girl Wing is transferred to the newborn nursery. 28.___
In examining Ms. Wing's episiotomy incision, which of these positions would be appropriate for the patient and would BEST help to minimize strain on the sutures?
A. Prone
B. Knee-chest
C. Sim's
D. Trendelenburg

29. Which of these measures, if carried out before Baby Girl Wing's discharge, will PROBABLY contribute to Ms. Wing's confidence in her ability to care for her baby? 29.___
A. Having Ms. Wing observe demonstrations of infant care in which equipment commonly found in the home is used
B. Having Ms. Wing take care of the baby in the hospital under the guidance of the registered nurse
C. Arranging for Mr. Wing to learn how to assist Ms. Wing with caring for the baby
D. Arranging to have the community health nurse visit with Ms. Wing and discuss areas that are of concern to Ms. Wing

30. Mr. and Ms. Wing discuss birth control with the nurse. 30.___
In selecting a method of birth control, the Wings should give priority to
A. Ms. Wing's age
B. the length of their marriage
C. the technique they find most acceptable
D. the success rate of a particular method

KEY (CORRECT ANSWERS)

1. D	11. B	21. D
2. D	12. C	22. A
3. B	13. D	23. A
4. A	14. C	24. D
5. C	15. C	25. A
6. B	16. D	26. B
7. B	17. C	27. D
8. A	18. C	28. C
9. B	19. B	29. B
10. B	20. D	30. C

EXAMINATION SECTION

DIRECTIONS FOR THIS SECTION:
Each question or incomplete statement is followed by several suggested answers or completions. Select the one that BEST answers the question or completes the statement. *PRINT THE LETTER OF THE CORRECT ANSWER IN THE SPACE AT THE RIGHT.*

TEST 1

1. Euphoria is a state of 1. ...
   A. depression B. elation C. ideation D. frustration
2. Salts affecting acidity or alkalinity of protoplasm have the effect of 2. ...
   A. osmosis B. condensation
   C. reduction D. buffer action
3. Cystitis means inflammation of the 3. ...
   A. kidneys B. cystic duct C. bladder D. urethra
4. A vesicant is an agent that is used to produce 4. ...
   A. fever B. relaxation C. lower pulse rate D. blisters
5. An ailment found *only* in older people is 5. ...
   A. maniac depression B. dementia praecox
   C. senile dementia D. tabes dorsalis
6. To keep a restless, semi-conscious patient from falling out of bed, we should use 6. ...
   A. heavy blankets stretched at the bedside, and pinned securely
   B. metal side boards C. restraint belts
   D. chairs at the exposed bed side
7. It is MOST important to see that reducing diets of adolescents do NOT lack 7. ...
   A. fats B. proteins
   C. carbohydrates D. simple sugars
8. For poisons, swallowed in capsule or tablet form, administer 8. ...
   A. a laxative B. warmth C. an emetic D. a stimulant
9. Oysters which feed on sewage sometimes transmit 9. ...
   A. rabies B. yellow fever C. malaria D. typhoid fever
10. Temperatures of 0°F. affect microbes to 10. ...
    A. stimulate mitosis B. check multiplication
    C. destroy them D. attenuate the cellular wall
11. The medium of infection over which the health authorities have LEAST control is 11. ...
    A. insects B. food C. water D. air
12. In case of sunstroke, the position of the head is 12. ...
    A. lowered, together with the shoulders
    B. elevated, together with the shoulders
    C. bent forward D. bent down, between the knees
13. An orthopedic aspect NOT usually found in cerebral palsy is 13. ...
    A. ataxia B. syndactylism C. athetosis D. rigidity
14. Encephalitis has NOT been associated with 14. ...
    A. infectious illnesses B. epidemics
    C. measles D. drugs

15. The Sulkowitch test of the urine tests for 15. ...
A. sodium B. potassium C. calcium D. chlorides

16. The presence of acetone in urine indicates faulty metabolism of 16. ...
A. proteins B. facts C. carbohydrates D. minerals

17. The test which aids the physician in confirming infectious mononucleosis is 17. ...
A. urinalysis B. Wasserman
C. sedimentation rate D. heterophile antibody test

18. The purpose of the therapeutic bath is to 18. ...
A. cool and refresh B. cleanse
C. induce sleep D. improve appearance

19. Syphilis is transmitted to the fetus through the 19. ...
A. ovum B. embryonic fluid C. placenta D. sperm

20. The permissive policy employed in some mental hospitals is associated with a(n) 20. ...
A. increase in assaultive behavior
B. open door policy
C. decrease in the use of physical restraint
D. increase in the use of physical restraint

21. A nurse can be of GREATEST help to the doctor by 21. ...
A. applying mental hygiene procedures
B. suggesting treatments
C. recording observations accurately
D. minimizing the patients' complaints

22. Some authorities believe that *all* pregnant women should be given gamma globulin to protect them from 22. ...
A. gonococcus B. German measles C. mumps D. chicken pox

23. BCG vaccine is used to increase resistance to 23. ...
A. poliomyelitis B. tuberculosis
C. smallpox D. mumps

24. In order to prevent rickets, the diet should include 24. ...
A. carotene B. calciferol C. riboflavin D. thiamin

25. To a dog bite wound, apply 25. ...
A. 2% iodine B. concentrated boric acid
C. carbolated vaseline D. running water

TEST 2

1. To prevent constipation in the aged, we should use 1. ...
A. enemas B. phenolthaleine
C. mineral oil D. proper diet

2. Sea food should be included in the diet at least once a week because of 2. ...
A. religion B. its iodine content
C. its iron content D. variety appeal

3. Baking soda added during the cooking of green vegetables to brighten their color, *also* acts to 3. ...
A. destroy vitamin content B. destroy texture effect
C. improve vitamin content D. improve flavor

4. The loop of Henle is a structural component of the 4. ...
A. aorta B. pulmones C. brain D. kidneys

5. At birth, the normal pulse rate per minute varies *between* 5. ...
A. 80-85 B. 90-95 C. 100-115 D. 120-150

6. Two potential killers in the home are 6. ...
   A. octachloro and methoxypromazine
   B. wax on milk containers and chlordane
   C. strontium 90 and nitrogen oxides
   D. polythylene and aminotriazole
7. Toxemia of pregnancy in diabetic mothers has been GREATLY reduced by the use of 7. ...
   A. iodine B. adrenalin C. hormones D. ergosterol
8. The body activity that is controlled CHIEFLY by the autonomic nervous system is 8. ...
   A. coughing B. peristalsis C. walking D. sneezing
9. The basal metabolism remains *unchanged* in a person with 9. ...
   A. nephritis B. malaria
   C. leukemia D. exophthalmic goiter
10. Excess glucose is removed from the blood stream by the 10. ...
    A. gall bladder B. liver C. small intestine D. pancreas
11. After proteins are digested, they are absorbed as 11. ...
    A. peptones B. fatty acids C. glycerol D. amino acids
12. The membrane which does NOT form part of the eyeball is the 12. ...
    A. conjunctiva B. sclera C. choroid D. retina
13. Upon discovering that a school child suffers from epilepsy, a teacher should notify the 13. ...
    A. principal B. bureau of child guidance
    C. bureau for physically handicapped
    D. department of health
14. The process which *increases* the vitamin D content of milk products is 14. ...
    A. homogenization B. condensation
    C. evaporation D. irradiation
15. A *good* source of amino acids is 15. ...
    A. carbohydrate B. fat C. protein D. citrus foods
16. For the patient, the MOST comfortable mattress protection is a 16. ...
    A. rubber draw sheet B. plastic pad
    C. quilted pad D. plastic contour "sheet"
17. To relieve the sensitive-skinned patient from bed pressure, use a(n) 17. ...
    A. inflated mattress B. inflated rubber ring
    C. cotton bandage ring D. sponge rubber ring
18. A symptom of dementia praecox is 18. ...
    A. extroversion B. tic paralysis
    C. unpredictability D. cerebral hemorrhage
19. A symptom of diabetes is 19. ...
    A. oliguria B. polyuria C. anuria D. hematuria
20. The disease characterized by the abnormal mitosis and development of body cells is 20. ...
    A. influenza B. Parkinson's disease
    C. carcinoma D. Graves' disease
21. The water used in preparing a mustard plaster should be 21. ...
    A. boiling B. cold C. tepid D. hot
22. In ear irrigation, the external ear is straightened by pulling the pinna 22. ...
    A. down and back B. down and forward
    C. up and forward D. up and back

23. To stimulate peristalsis, the fluid in colonic irrigation should be 23. ...
A. cool B. lukewarm C. warm D. hot
24. Substituting an activity in which a person can succeed for one in which he may fail, is termed 24. ...
A. sublimation B. projection
C. rationalization D. compensation
25. Rationalization is the result of 25. ...
A. believing what one wants to believe
B. reflective thinking C. scientific thinking
D. basing conclusions on fact

TEST 3

1. Delusions of persecution are *typical* of 1. ...
A. epilepsy B. regression C. schizophrenia D. paranoia
2. A person with an IQ of 85 would be classified as 2. ...
A. defective B. normal C. dull average D. borderline
3. Ultra-violet rays harm the eyes by 3. ...
A. drying out mucous B. enlarging the pupil
C. spotting the cornea D. destroying visual purple
4. The sclera and choroid tissues are found in the 4. ...
A. ear B. heart C. eye D. stomach
5. Hypoglycemia indicates the need for the administration of 5. ...
A. adrenalin B. a simple sugar
C. insulin D. salt
6. To reduce swelling, apply 6. ...
A. hot applications B. cold applications
C. electric heating pad D. a snug bandage
7. The value of antihistaminic compounds lies *primarily* in their ability to 7. ...
A. prevent the spread of infection
B. relieve the allergic manifestations
C. lessen the number of infections
D. immunize
8. Very hot and very cold foods, fed to a patient with acute mycardial infarction, can cause irregular heart beat by irritating the 8. ...
A. median nerve B. common peronal nerve
C. deep peronal nerve D. vagus nerve
9. The mineral which maintains osmotic pressure in the human system is 9. ...
A. iron B. potassium C. magnesium D. sodium
10. Dishes used by a patient with a communicable disease should be 10. ...
A. boiled for 5 minutes in soapy water
B. boiled in a creosote solution
C. washed in clear water at 180°F.
D. washed for 5 minutes in soapy hot water
11. Incineration of infectious material means 11. ...
A. disinfecting B. burning C. washing D. boiling
12. Tachycardia is *also* known as 12. ...
A. high blood pressure B. low blood pressure
C. rapid pulse D. slow pulse

13. Dyspnea is 13. ...
    A. blurring vision B. pain around the heart
    C. difficult breathing D. discoloration of the skin
14. *Manifest deviation* of one eye when looking at an object is called 14. ...
    A. strabismus B. astigmatism
    C. accommodation D. glaucoma
15. Abnormally slow pulse is referred to as 15. ...
    A. tachycardia B. intermittent
    C. arrhythmia D. brachycardia
16. The natural source of insulin is the 16. ...
    A. liver B. thymus gland C. pineal gland D. pancreas
17. Dilation is a medication used in the treatment of 17. ...
    A. cardiac involvement B. multiple sclerosis
    C. grand mal D. cerebral palsy
18. The MOST practical bed sheet is made of 18. ...
    A. muslin B. broadcloth C. nylon D. linen
19. Contaminated equipment should be cleared of spore formers by 19. ...
    A. soaking in strong acid B. refrigerating
    C. dessicating D. intermittent autoclaving
20. Decubitus is another name for 20. ...
    A. mental derangement B. dyspnea
    C. decayed teeth D. bedsore
21. Of the following, the *non-infectious* disease is 21. ...
    A. hepatitis B. poliomyelitis C. diabetes D. impetigo
22. The CHIEF purpose of isolating a patient is to 22. ...
    A. protect others B. prevent reinfection
    C. hasten recovery D. provide peace and comfort
23. Excessive amounts of alcoholic beverages over a period of time 23. ...
    A. hamper the production of gastric juices
    B. reduce nervous anxiety
    C. dilate the blood vessels D. increase mental alertness
24. In giving first-aid treatment to a person who has fainted, 24. ...
    A. administer a hot beverage
    B. hold the head back and open the mouth
    C. administer aromatic spirits of ammonia
    D. lower the head below heart level
25. The law which attempts to control the distribution of drugs is the 25. ...
    A. Wagner Act B. McCarran Act
    C. Harrison Act D. Taft-Hartley Act

TEST 4

1. The MOST harmful drug derived from opium is 1. ...
    A. heroin B. morphine C. cocaine D. codeine
2. Novocain is derived from the 2. ...
    A. coca plant B. poppy plant
    C. hemp plant D. ergot fungus
3. A drug which is a substitute for morphine in the treatment of drug addiction is 3. ...
    A. codein B. demerol C. pantapon D. methadone

4. The drug having LEAST narcotic effect per unit of weight is 4. ...
   A. marijuana B. cocaine C. opium D. barbiturates
5. Nissel's granules are found in the 5. ...
   A. kidney B. heart C. brain D. lung
6. An hypnotic drug which does NOT initiate drug addiction is 6. ...
   A. dormison B. sodium amytal
   C. sodium phenobarbital D. seconal
7. The United States Public Health Service Hospitals for drug addicts are in the cities of 7. ...
   A. Chicago, Illinois, and Detroit, Michigan
   B. Lexington, Kentucky, and Fort Worth, Texas
   C. Cleveland, Ohio, and Ames, Iowa
   D. Salina, Kansas, and Delmonte, California
8. A term meaning "far-sightedness" is 8. ...
   A. hyperopia B. nystagmus
   C. strabismus D. myopia
9. Cholecystrography is the x-ray examination of the 9. ...
   A. stomach B. spleen C. gall bladder D. intestines
10. Pyelonephritis is an inflammation of the 10. ...
    A. kidney B. pancreas C. rectum D. mastoid
11. Pellagra results from a deficiency of 11. ...
    A. ascorbic acid B. thiamine C. riboflavin D. niacin
12. Cheilosis results from a deficiency of 12. ...
    A. pyrodoxin B. vitamin E C. riboflavin D. niacin
13. In a healthy young woman, the prenatal period is *USUALLY* a time of 13. ...
    A. well being B. semi-invalidism
    C. chronic disability D. extreme emotionalism
14. The food substance which, when absorbed by the body, is MOST likely to increase the colloidal osmotic pressure of the blood, is 14. ...
    A. carbohydrates B. fats C. glucoses D. proteins
15. An acid ash is yielded by body oxidation of 15. ...
    A. meats B. citrus fruits C. potatoes D. cream
16. A precursor of vitamin A is 16. ...
    A. ergosterol B. carotene C. lysine D. pyrodoxine
17. The term describing physical symptoms that do not arise *entirely* from physical causes is 17. ...
    A. organic B. psychoneurotic
    C. psychosomatic D. psychopathological
18. The mechanism of attributing one's own ideas to others is termed 18. ...
    A. projection B. substitution
    C. sublimation D. rationalization
19. A child's tendency to pattern after his parents is known as 19. ...
    A. identification B. projection
    C. compensation D. substitution
20. Stuttering in children *usually* originates from 20. ...
    A. physical handicap B. mentally deficient parents
    C. emotional conflict D. imitation of other stutterers
21. Folic acid, used in the treatment of pernicious anemia, must be given with vitamin 21. ...
    A. B_1 B. B_2 C. B_6 D. B_{12}
22. Radioactive iodine compound is fed to determine the 22. ...
    A. site of red blood cell production

B. incidence of anemia C. presence of cholesterol
D. thyroid activity

23. Predisposition to epilepsy may be discovered through the use of the 23. ...
A. stethoscope B. fluoroscope
C. encephalograph D. opthalmoscope

24. An *early* symptom of glaucoma is 24. ...
A. blindness B. gradual loss of side vision
C. excessive tearing D. cataract formation

25. A kind of nervous headache *USUALLY* periodical and confined to one side of the head is 25. ...
A. pressure B. vertigo C. migraine D. traumatic

TEST 5

1. For terminal disinfection of thermometers, soak them in a solution of 1. ...
A. 90% alcohol B. merthiolate
C. mercurochrome D. boric acid

2. A child who has been in contact with a known case of measles may be considered safe *after* 2. ...
A. 10 days B. 40 days C. 7 days D. 21 days

3. The drug *often* used in shock therapy is 3. ...
A. metrazol B. dicumerol C. dilantin D. insulin

4. First-aid care of a third-degree burn requires 4. ...
A. an ointment B. a sterile dressing
C. opening of the blisters D. an antiseptic solution

5. The *usual* reason why an infant spits out food is that it 5. ...
A. dislikes the unfamiliar taste
B. prefers liquids C. is obstinate
D. has not learned to swallow soft foods

6. The BEST time to introduce new foods is when the child 6. ...
A. has learned to obey
B. understands it is good for him
C. is very hungry D. is very happy

7. The patient should be kept warm because the blood then 7. ...
A. *increases* in viscosity B. *decreases* in viscosity
C. *decreases* in fluidity D. *increases* in saline content

8. Pure ammonia solution is 8. ...
A. alkaline B. acid C. neutral D. saline

9. In a reducing diet, use high protein content because protein has 9. ...
A. high satiety value B. low caloric value
C. low specific dynamic action D. easy availability

10. Dextrose-maltose is *valuable* in infant formulae because it increases 10. ...
A. homogenization B. digestibility
C. palatability D. carbohydrate content

11. The substances that are *non-miscible* are 11. ...
A. linseed oil and lime water
B. soap and water C. glycerin and alcohol
D. olive oil and acetic acid

12. The PRIMARY host for bacteria causing undulant fever is the 12. ...
A. dog B. goat C. cow D. fox

13. Blood clotting is *initiated* by 13. ...
  A. fibrinogen B. thromboplastin
  C. calcium ions D. vitamin K
14. When using the terminal heat method in preparing baby's formula, 14. ...
  A. cover utensils and boil for three minutes
  B. sterilize utensils and formula before bottling
  C. sterilize the bottles
  D. stand utensils and bottles in boiling water for thirty minutes
15. The MOST accurate way to measure liquid medicine is to use a 15. ...
  A. standard teaspoon B. standard medicine glass
  C. glass kitchen measuring cup
  D. six-ounce drinking glass
16. In preparing an ice bag, use 16. ...
  A. half ice, half water
  B. enough ice to half fill the bag
  C. enough ice to fill the bag D. about one pound of ice
17. Acute intoxication may be a psychosis because it produces 17. ...
  A. severe loss of contact with reality
  B. intellectual limitations
  C. emotional inadequacies D. bodily diseases
18. The substance known as ACTH is a secretion of 18. ...
  A. adrenal cortex B. thyroid
  C. anterior pituitary D. pancreas
19. Morphine 1/4 grain administered 45 minutes before surgery is intended to serve as a 19. ...
  A. respiratory depressant B. hemotinic
  C. diuretic D. hypnotic
20. The tissue in which infection spreads rapidly is 20. ...
  A. adipose B. fibrous C. areolar D. reticular
21. Boiling in water for ten minutes will destroy 21. ...
  A. non-spore forming microbes B. spore-forming microbes
  C. spore-forming pathogens D. pathogens
22. The temperature of the child under four years of age should be taken by 22. ...
  A. mouth B. rectum
  C. axilla D. either by mouth or axilla
23. When putting drops into the eyes of a patient, 23. ...
  A. drop them on the eyeball B. drop onto the lower lid
  C. use the medication in an eyecup
  D. drop them into the inner corner
24. The *safe* temperature for water in a hot-water bottle for an adult with a normal skin is 24. ...
  A. 140°-145°F. B. 120°-130°F.
  C. 100°-125°F. D. 110°-115°F.
25. If a child does NOT eat his meal, 25. ...
  A. remind him to eat
  B. amuse him while he eats
  C. remove the food until next meal time
  D. remove the food until he asks for it

TEST 6

1. The PRINCIPAL way in which germs enter the body is through 1. ...
   A. skin breaks B. sex organs
   C. nose and mouth D. eye or ear
2. Normal feeding habits develop if parents 2. ...
   A. gently force the child to eat
   B. stress good manners every meal
   C. prepare food by mashing and mixing it well
   D. offer adequate food in a matter-of-fact way, without urging
3. Fluorination of community water is 3. ...
   A. definitely unsafe
   B. still in early experimental stage
   C. safe beyond reasonable doubt
   D. harmless but of little value
4. Simple goiter may be caused by lack of 4. ...
   A. calcium B. phosphorus C. iodine D. sodium
5. The diet in nephritic edema should be 5. ...
   A. high in vitamins and fluids
   B. low in proteins and fats
   C. high in proteins and minerals
   D. low in fluids and minerals
6. In first-aid treatment of nosebleed in a young child, permit the child to 6. ...
   A. lie flat on his back
   B. sit in a chair, tip head back, apply cold compresses
   C. sit up, head forward, apply cold compress at nostrils and back of neck
   D. blow nose, then press nostrils shut
7. MOST finger stains may be removed from wall paper with 7. ...
   A. benzene B. soap and water
   C. art gum D. heat and brown paper
8. The "dominating gland" or master glad of all the endocrine glands is the 8. ...
   A. anterior lobe of the pituitary B. pineal body
   C. adrenal cortex D. spleen
9. A *non-communicable* disease is 9. ...
   A. syphilis B. pneumonia C. carcinoma D. typhus fever
10. The physiological stimulant for the respiratory center is 10. ...
    A. oxygen B. calcium ions
    C. carbon dioxide D. lactic acid
11. The MINIMUM time in which dishes may be disinfected by boiling in water is 11. ...
    A. 15 minutes B. 10 minutes C. 5 minutes D. 2 minutes
12. Dichloro-diphenyl-trichoroethane is used extensively because it 12. ...
    A. retains residual effectiveness
    B. is non-toxic to handlers C. does not burn
    D. dissolves in water
13. The disease that is transmitted by an insect is 13. ...
    A. diphtheria B. typhus fever
    C. scarlet fever D. poliomyelitis
14. For lumbar punctures, the needle is *usually* introduced just 14. ...
    A. *above* the first lumbar vertebra
    B. *below* the last lumbar vertebra

C. *above* the last lumbar vertebra
D. *below* the first lumbar vertebra

15. Antigens used to stimulate active immunity are called 15. ...
A. serums B. vaccines C. inoculations D. injections
16. Keratitis is an inflammation of the 16. ...
A. cornea B. iris C. fundus D. lachrymal ducts
17. The soft part of the tooth that is susceptible to decay is the 17. ..
A. pulp B. dentine C. crown D. root
18. A child with "growing pains" should be 18. ...
A. examined physically B. hospitalized
C. told to forget them
D. watched carefully for a few weeks
19. The unit used for measuring acuity of hearing is the 19. ...
A. otometer B. decibel
C. audiometer D. auditory ossicle
20. Inflammation of the tear sac is called 20. ...
A. dacrocystitis B. cystitis
C. iritis D. cyclitis
21. The method advocated for treating skeletal tuberculosis includes 21. ...
A. bed rest and plenty of fresh air
B. spinal fusion operation
C. placing patient on a rigid frame
D. antibiotic therapy, rest and surgery
22. A mustard plaster for an adult with a normal skin should have a mixture of mustard and flour, respectively, in the proportion of one to 22. ...
A. two B. six C. ten D. twelve
23. A child activity that encourages social contacts is a 23. ...
A. picture book B. sandpile
C. soft woolly toy dog D. a toy piano
24. The baby's FIRST toy should be something to 24. ...
A. hold B. watch as it moves C. chew on D. pound
25. In illness, the importance of sunshine lies CHIEFLY in the fact that it 25. ...
A. induces relaxation B. supplies vitamin D
C. increases morale D. is a powerful disinfectant

TEST 7

1. The nurse rubs the patient's back with alcohol in order to 1. ...
A. kill germs on the patient's skin
B. relax the muscles and prevent bed sores
C. speed the cure D. keep the patient clean
2. When a prescribed medicine is no longer required, it should be 2. ...
A. saved for the next illness
B. disposed of in the garbage or down the drain
C. given to another patient with a similar illness
D. administered until all is consumed
3. The *purpose* of the therapeutic bath is to 3. ...
A. cool and refresh B. cleanse
C. induce sleep D. improve appearance

4. The change of nutrients into protoplasm is 4. ...
   A. anabolism B. karyokinesis
   C. osmosis D. catabolism
5. The *preferred* method for administering cough medicine is 5. ...
   A. from the medicine glass B. mixed with water
   C. from a spoon D. through a siphon tube
6. The MOST effective means of lowering the death rate from cancer is 6. ...
   A. radium treatment B. x-ray treatment
   C. early diagnosis D. surgery
7. The FIRST attack of rheumatic fever results in a child being 7. ...
   A. immune to further attacks B. permanently crippled
   C. subject to further attacks
   D. certain to have heart complications
8. The hereditary disease in which blood does NOT clot properly is 8. ...
   A. anemia B. leukemia C. hemophilia D. amoebiosis
9. In first aid, a penetrating foreign body in the eyeball should be treated by 9. ...
   A. removing the object B. applying a loose bandage
   C. sending the patient to a doctor
   D. applying a snug bandage
10. The effect of heat on the vasodilator is to 10. ...
   A. stimulate B. deteriorate C. stabilize D. inhibit
11. A stroke is a(n) 11. ...
   A. cerebral hemorrhage B. sinus thrombosis
   C. cerebral dystrophy D. aneurism
12. Painful effects of arthritis may be caused by 12. ...
   A. chilling winds
   B. toxins from a disease germ
   C. complications of an infectious disease
   D. air conditioning
13. In diabetes, the body is unable to utilize 13. ...
   A. vitamins B. proteins C. fats D. carbohydrates
14. The aged bed patient is likely to have bed sores because he 14. ...
   A. is uncooperative
   B. lies in one position and has poor circulation
   C. limits his diet D. is uncomfortable
15. The thinking of an alcoholic becomes compulsive about 15. ...
   A. the next drink B. abstinence
   C. violence D. the need for relaxation
16. The *normal* inspiration rate per minute for the healthy adult is 16. ...
   A. 8-12 B. 16-20 C. 24-28 D. 30-35
17. Anemia is determined by 17. ...
   A. color of skin B. laboratory techniques
   C. undue fatigue D. dizziness without apparent cause
18. The aged citizen is BEST cared for in 18. ...
   A. the home environment B. old age homes
   C. hospitals for the aged
   D. a town developed for old people
19. The outside leaves of salad greens are important because they 19. ...
   A. make the salad crispy B. are larger

C. have more color D. contain more vitamin A and iron

20. Rubber goods should be stored in a 20. ...
A. cool dry place B. tin container
C. medicine cabinet D. warm, moist place

21. Caffeine and strychnine stimulate the 21. ...
A. brain and afferent nerves B. brain and spinal cord
C. autonomic ganglia and efferent nerves
D. hepatic and pulmonary nerves

22. To get the required amount of vitamin C, consume 22. ...
A. cole slaw B. cocoa
C. apricots D. whole wheat bread

23. Hyperfunution of the islands of Langerhans may cause 23. ...
A. hypoliposis B. hemorrhage
C. hypoglycemia D. hypostalic congestion

24. Osteomalacia is 24. ...
A. bony tumor B. softening of the bones
C. inflammation of bone marrow D. formation of bone

25. Asphyxiation may be caused by 25. ...
A. heavy concentration of alcohol in the blood stream
B. consuming alcohol on an empty stomach
C. mixing more than one kind of alcoholic drink
D. taking sedatives while drinking

TEST 8

1. An incision of the colon for the purpose of making a fistula is an operation termed 1. ...
A. colostration B. colostomy
C. Mikulicz operation D. gastrostomy

2. "Mainliner" is a drug addict who uses the drug for 2. ...
A. smoking B. snorting
C. intra-muscular injection D. intra-venal injection

3. Bright's disease is *also* called 3. ...
A. hepatitis B. nephritis
C. Paget's disease D. otitis

4. Anodyne refers to a medication that 4. ...
A. counteracts or removes the effect of poison
B. relieves pain C. prevents the growth of germs
D. prolongs the life of red blood cells

5. Common symptoms of shock are 5. ...
A. slow pulse, flushed skin B. slow pulse, bright eyes
C. pale skin, bright eyes D. pale, clammy skin

6. The CHIEF value of cellulose in the diet is that it 6. ...
A. is more soluble than starch
B. gives bulk to the intestinal residues
C. is easily digested
D. provides an essential amino acid

7. Adult dietary protein requirements are determined PRIMARILY by 7. ...
A. age and weight B. climatic conditions
C. body weight in relation to age and height
D. muscular activity

8. The purpose of insuring regular rate of respiration is to reduce the amount of 8. ...
   A. water in the body
   B. blood passing through the aorta
   C. carbon dioxide in the blood
   D. iron in the red blood cells
9. Treatment of generalized arteriosclerosis is through 9. ...
   A. bed rest B. moderation in living
   C. drugs D. dealing with the aging process
10. Prolonged administration of narcotics is MOST likely to result in the 10. ...
    A. need for increased dosage
    B. reduction of physical resistance
    C. development of aggressiveness
    D. addiction or craving for the drug
11. Rugs and carpets should be removed from the sick room because they 11. ...
    A. collect dust and germs
    B. increase the work in cleaning
    C. produce a static when walked on
    D. present a hazard
12. The administration of narcotics in the hospital is by the 12. ...
    A. doctor B. nurse C. pharmacist D. aide
13. Of the following, the factor contributing MOST to apoplexy is 13. ...
    A. coronary thrombosis B. aphasia
    C. low blood pressure D. high blood pressure
14. Croup responds MOST quickly to administrations of 14. ...
    A. pertussin medication B. special diet
    C. steam inhalations D. restricted physical movement
15. It is CORRECT to state that enzymes 15. ...
    A. are used up in chemical reactions of foods
    B. retard the process of breaking down of foods
    C. work only in acid surroundings
    D. are specific in their action

16. Of PRIME importance in training children is 16. ...
    A. mild punishment B. scolding for deviate behavior
    C. consistency of treatment
    D. ignoring undesirable behavior
17. In the destruction of microbes, the effect of heat is to produce 17. ...
    A. liquefaction B. asphyxiation
    C. coagulation D. precipitation
18. Hutchinson's teeth are an indication of 18. ...
    A. rickets B. congenital syphilis
    C. rheumatic heart disease D. nutritional anemia

19. A drug *often* used in the prevention and treatment of motion sickness is 19. ...
    A. dramamine B. streptomycin
    C. atropin D. aureomycin
20. The substance which is NOT a constituent of normal urine is 20. ...
    A. ammonia B. creatinine C. hippuric acid D. indican

21. To reduce fear in children, parents should 21. ...
    A. extend affection B. explain each request
    C. keep them under close supervision
    D. provide safeguards
22. When a child is believed to be suffering with a communicable disease, it is the responsibility of the school to 22. ...
    A. send him home B. send him to a doctor
    C. isolate him
    D. report the matter to the administrative office
23. The GREATEST production care is given to milk that is labeled 23. ...
    A. pasteurized B. approved Grade A
    C. homogenized D. certified
24. Of the following, the MOST common cause of death today is 24. ...
    A. cancer B. diabetes C. heart disease D. pneumonia
25. Lipase converts 25. ...
    A. fats into fatty acids B. fats into proteoses
    C. proteins into amino acids D. sugars into fructose

TEST 9

1. First aid care of a third degree burn requires 1. ...
   A. oil and chalk mixture B. antiseptic solution
   C. sterile dressing D. healing ointment
2. Heat destroys bacteria by 2. ...
   A. enucleation B. coagulating protein
   C. hemolysis D. making the cell wall permeable
3. The process by which digested food enters the blood stream is known as 3. ...
   A. assimilation B. catabolism
   C. osmosis D. anabolism
4. The control of automatic breathing is located in the 4. ...
   A. cerebellum B. cerebrum
   C. amnion D. medulla oblongata
5. Difficulty in speaking is known as 5. ...
   A. anorexia B. amnesia C. aphasia D. asphyxia
6. Drug withdrawal symptoms in addicts are vomiting and changes in 6. ...
   A. muscular control B. color of the skin
   C. nerves D. pupils of the eyes
7. Croup responds MOST quickly to 7. ...
   A. steam inhalations B. a balanced diet
   C. cough syrup D. bed rest
8. The organ MOST commonly affected by arteriosclerosis is the 8. ...
   A. brain B. lung C. kidney D. heart
9. The position of the head for treatment in a case of "sunstroke" is 9. ...
   A. lowered on to the chest B. lowered between the knees
   C. elevated together with the shoulders
   D. elevated in erect position
10. Radioactive iodine compound is fed to a patient to determine the 10. ...
    A. site of red blood cell production
    B. incidence of anemia C. presence of cholesterol
    D. activity of the thyroid

11. Doctors and nurses are required to treat ophthalmia neonatorium with 11. ...
    A. penicillin B. sulfacetamide
    C. silver nitrate D. sulphathiozole
12. The administration of drugs in the hospital is *usually* by the 12. ...
    A. doctor B. nurse C. pharmacist D. aide
13. The care of the mouth thermometer after use is by *immediately* 13. ...
    A. soaking for 5 minutes in an antiseptic solution
    B. soaping and rinsing alternately twice and carefully drying
    C. storing in alcohol D. washing under running water
14. An alcohol sponge bath reduces an elevated temperature because 14. ...
    A. the odor is refreshing
    B. it removes moisture from the skin surface
    C. it absorbs heat by evaporation
    D. the sting stimulates the skin
15. In city schools, every school child MUST be immunized against 15. ...
    A. whooping cough B. polio
    C. small pox D. diphtheria
16. Skeletal tuberculosis is treated by 16. ...
    A. bed rest and plenty of fresh air
    B. spinal fusion surgery
    C. rigorous antibiotic therapy combined with rest and possible surgery
    D. restraint of spinal movement
17. A child with "growing pains" should be 17. ...
    A. encouraged to disregard them
    B. hospitalized at once
    C. observed carefully for a week before attempting remedy
    D. sent for a physical examination
18. Some carbohydrates are required in a diabetic diet in order that 18. ...
    A. sugars may be avoided B. fats may be oxidized
    C. loss of weight may be prevented
    D. intestinal putrefaction may be reduced
19. The diet of a 72-year-old obese woman should include *extra* quantities of 19. ...
    A. proteins B. vitamins C. carbohydrates D. minerals
20. ACTH is a secretion of the 20. ...
    A. parathyroid B. adrenal cortex
    C. anterior pituitary D. thyroid
21. Blood clotting is *accelerated* by the administration of 21. ...
    A. fibrinogen B. vitamin K
    C. calcium carbonate D. thromboplastin
22. The COMMONEST cause of death in the United States today is 22. ...
    A. cancer B. heart disease C. diabetes D. pneumonia
23. A "stroke" is one of the effects of 23. ...
    A. cerebral dystrophy B. aneurysm
    C. cerebral hemorrhage D. sinus thrombosis
24. Inability to write, due to a brain lesion, is known as 24. ...
    A. agraphia B. aphasia C. aproxia D. anorexia

25. Marijuana is obtained from the 25. ...
   A. hemp plant B. thorn apple
   C. coca shrub D. nightshade plant

KEYS (CORRECT ANSWERS)

	TEST 1	TEST 2	TEST 3	TEST 4	TEST 5	TEST 6	TEST 7	TEST 8	TEST 9
1.	B	D	D	A	B	C	B	B	C
2.	D	B	C	A	D	D	B	D	B
3.	C	A	D	D	D	C	A	B	C
4.	D	D	C	A	B	C	D	B	D
5.	C	D	B	C	D	D	C	D	C
6.	B	D	B	A	D	C	C	B	D
7.	B	C	B	B	B	C	C	C	A
8.	C	B	D	A	A	A	C	C	C
9.	D	A	D	C	A	C	B	B	C
10.	B	B	A	A	D	C	A	D	D
11.	D	D	B	D	D	C	A	D	C
12.	B	A	C	C	B	A	B	B	B
13.	B	A	C	A	B	B	D	D	D
14.	D	D	A	D	B	D	B	C	C
15.	C	C	D	A	B	B	A	D	C
16.	C	C	D	B	B	A	B	C	C
17.	D	A	C	C	A	B	B	C	D
18.	A	C	A	A	C	A	A	B	B
19.	C	B	D	A	D	B	D	A	B
20.	B	C	D	C	C	A	A	D	C
21.	C	C	C	D	A	D	B	A	D
22.	B	D	A	D	B	B	A	A	B
23.	B	A	A	C	B	B	C	D	C
24.	B	D	D	B	B	B	B	C	A
25.	D	A	C	C	C	D	A	A	A

EXAMINATION SECTION

TEST 1

DIRECTIONS: Each question or incomplete statement is followed by several suggested answers or completions. Select the one that BEST answers the question or completes the statement. *PRINT THE LETTER OF THE CORRECT ANSWER IN THE SPACE AT THE RIGHT.*

1. For terminal disinfection of thermometers, soak them in a solution of 1.___
   A. 90% alcohol B. merthiolate
   C. mercurochrome D. boric acid

2. Pure ammonia solution is 2.___
   A. alkaline B. acid C. neutral D. saline

3. In a reducing diet, use high protein content because protein has 3.___
   A. high satiety value
   B. low calorie value
   C. low specific dynamic action
   D. easy availability

4. Dextro-maltose is valuable in infant formulae because it increases 4.___
   A. homogenization B. digestibility
   C. palatability D. carbohydrate content

5. The substances that are non-miscible are 5.___
   A. linseed oil and lime water
   B. soap and water
   C. glycerin and alcohol
   D. olive oil and acetic acid

6. The substance known as *ACTH* is a secretion of 6.___
   A. adrenal cortex B. thyroid
   C. anterior pituitary D. pancreas

7. The tissue in which infection spreads rapidly is 7.___
   A. adipose B. fibrous C. areolar D. reticular

8. Boiling in water for ten minutes will destroy 8.___
   A. non-spore forming microbes
   B. spore-forming microbes
   C. spore-forming pathogens
   D. pathogens

9. The PRINCIPAL way in which germs enter the body is through 9.___
   A. skin breaks B. sex organs
   C. nose and mouth D. eye or ear

10. Fluorination of community water is 10.___
    A. definitely unsafe
    B. still in early experimental stage
    C. safe beyond reasonable doubt
    D. harmless but of little value

11. Simple goiter may be caused by lack of 11.___
    A. calcium B. phosphorus C. iodine D. sodium

12. MOST finger stains may be removed from wallpaper with 12.___
    A. benzene B. soap and water
    C. art gum D. heat and brown paper

13. The *dominating gland* or master gland of all the endocrine glands is the 13.___
    A. anterior lobe of the pituitary
    B. pineal body
    C. adrenal cortex
    D. spleen

14. The physiological stimulant for the respiratory center is 14.___
    A. oxygen B. calcium ions
    C. carbon dioxide D. lactic acid

15. The MINIMUM time in which dishes may be disinfected by boiling in water is _____ minutes. 15.___
    A. 15 B. 10 C. 5 D. 2

16. Dichloro-diphenyl-trichoroethane is used extensively because it 16.___
    A. retains residual effectiveness
    B. is non-toxic to handlers
    C. does not burn
    D. dissolves in water

17. For lumbar punctures, the needle is USUALLY introduced just _____ the _____ lumbar vertebra. 17.___
    A. above; first B. below; last
    C. above; last D. below; first

18. Antigens used to stimulate active immunity are called 18.___
    A. serums B. vaccines
    C. inoculations D. injections

19. The soft part of the tooth that is susceptible to decay is the 19.___
    A. pulp B. dentine C. crown D. root

20. The unit used for measuring acuity of hearing is the 20.___
    A. otometer B. decibel
    C. audiometer D. auditory ossicle

21. A mustard plaster for an adult with a normal skin should have a mixture of mustard and flour, respectively, in the proportion of one to 21.___
    A. two B. six C. ten D. twelve

22. In illness, the importance of sunshine lies CHIEFLY in the fact that it 22.___
   A. induces relaxation
   B. supplies vitamin D
   C. increases morale
   D. is a powerful disinfectant

23. The change of nutrients into protoplasm is 23.___
   A. anabolism B. karyokinesis
   C. osmosis D. catabolism

24. The effect of heat on the vasodilator is to 24.___
   A. stimulate B. deteriorate
   C. stabilize D. inhibit

25. Painful effects of arthritis may be caused by 25.___
   A. chilling winds
   B. toxins from a disease germ
   C. complications of an infectious disease
   D. air conditioning

KEY (CORRECT ANSWERS)

1. B	11. C
2. A	12. C
3. A	13. A
4. D	14. C
5. D	15. C
6. C	16. A
7. C	17. D
8. A	18. B
9. C	19. B
10. C	20. B

21. B
22. D
23. D
24. A
25. B

TEST 2

DIRECTIONS: Each question or incomplete statement is followed by several suggested answers or completions. Select the one that BEST answers the question or completes the statement. *PRINT THE LETTER OF THE CORRECT ANSWER IN THE SPACE AT THE RIGHT.*

1. In diabetes, the body is unable to utilize 1.___
   A. vitamins B. proteins
   C. fats D. carbohydrates

2. The NORMAL inspiration rate per minute for the healthy adult is 2.___
   A. 8-12 B. 16-20 C. 24-28 D. 30-35

3. The outside leaves of salad greens are important because they 3.___
   A. make the salad crispy
   B. are larger
   C. have more color
   D. contain more vitamin A and iron

4. Rubber goods should be stored in a 4.___
   A. cool dry place B. tin container
   C. medicine cabinet D. warm, moist place

5. Caffeine and strychnine stimulate the 5.___
   A. brain and afferent nerves
   B. brain and spinal cord
   C. autonomic ganglia and efferent nerves
   D. hepatic and pulmonary nerves

6. To get the required amount of vitamin C, consume 6.___
   A. cole slaw B. cocoa
   C. apricots D. whole wheat bread

7. Hyperfunction of the islands of Langerhans may cause 7.___
   A. hypoliposis B. hemorrhage
   C. hypoglycemia D. hypostalic congestion

8. The purpose of insuring regular rate of respiration is to reduce the amount of 8.___
   A. water in the body
   B. blood passing through the aorta
   C. carbon dioxide in the blood
   D. iron in the red blood cells

9. In destruction of microbes, the effect of heat is to produce 9.___
   A. liquefaction B. asphyxiation
   C. coagulation D. precipitation

10. The substance which is NOT a constituent of normal urine is 10.____
A. ammonia B. creatinine
C. hippuric acid D. indican

11. The GREATEST production care is given to milk that is labeled 11.____
A. pasteurized B. approved Grade A
C. homogenized D. certified

12. Lipase converts _____ into _____. 12.____
A. fats; fatty acids B. fats; proteoses
C. proteins; amino acids D. sugars; fructose

13. Salts affecting acidity or alkalinity of protoplasm have the effect of 13.____
A. osmosis B. condensation
C. reduction D. buffer action

14. Temperatures of 0°F affect microbes to 14.____
A. stimulate mitosis B. check multiplication
C. destroy them D. attenuate the cellular wall

15. Baking soda added during the cooking of green vegetables to brighten their color also acts to 15.____
A. destroy vitamin content B. destroy texture effect
C. improve vitamin content D. improve flavor

16. The loop of Henle is a structural component of the 16.____
A. aorta B. pulmones C. brain D. kidneys

17. Two potential killers in the home to which the public has been alerted by the Department of Health, Education and Welfare are 17.____
A. octachloro and methoxypromazine
B. wax on milk containers and chlordane
C. strontium 90 and nitrogen oxides
D. polyethylene and aminotriazole

18. The body activity that is controlled CHIEFLY by the autonomic nervous system is 18.____
A. coughing B. peristalsis
C. walking D. sneezing

19. The basal metabolism remains unchanged in a person with 19.____
A. nephritis B. malaria
C. leukemia D. exophthalmic goiter

20. Excess glucose is removed from the bloodstream by the 20.____
A. gall bladder B. liver
C. small intestine D. pancreas

21. After proteins are digested, they are absorbed as 21.____
A. peptones B. fatty acids
C. glycerol D. amino acids

22. The membrane which does NOT form part of the eyeball is the 22.___
    A. conjunctiva B. sclera
    C. choroid D. retina

23. The process which increases the vitamin D content of milk products is 23.___
    A. homogenization B. condensing
    C. evaporation D. irradiation

24. A GOOD source of amino acids is 24.___
    A. carbohydrate B. fat
    C. protein D. citrus foods

25. Ultra-violet rays harm the eyes by 25.___
    A. drying out mucous B. enlarging the pupil
    C. spotting the cornea D. destroying visual purple

KEY (CORRECT ANSWERS)

1. D
2. B
3. D
4. A
5. B

6. A
7. C
8. C
9. C
10. D

11. D
12. A
13. D
14. B
15. A

16. D
17. D
18. B
19. A
20. B

21. D
22. A
23. D
24. C
25. D

TEST 3

DIRECTIONS: Each question or incomplete statement is followed by several suggested answers or completions. Select the one that BEST answers the question or completes the statement. *PRINT THE LETTER OF THE CORRECT ANSWER IN THE SPACE AT THE RIGHT.*

1. The sclera and chorioid tissues are found in the 1.____
   A. ear B. heart C. eye D. stomach

2. The mineral which maintains osmotic pressure in the human system is 2.____
   A. iron B. potassium C. magnesium D. sodium

3. Dishes used by a patient with a communicable disease should be 3.____
   A. boiled for 5 minutes in soapy water
   B. boiled in a creosote solution
   C. washed in clear water at 180°F
   D. washed for 5 minutes in soapy hot water

4. The natural source of insulin is the 4.____
   A. liver B. thymus gland
   C. pineal gland D. pancreas

5. Contaminated equipment should be cleared of spore formers by 5.____
   A. soaking in strong acid B. refrigerating
   C. dessicating D. intermittent autoclaving

6. Excessive amounts of alcoholic beverages over a period of time 6.____
   A. hamper the production of gastric juices
   B. reduce nervous anxiety
   C. dilate the blood vessels
   D. increase mental alertness

7. The MOST harmful drug derived from opium is 7.____
   A. heroin B. morphine C. cocaine D. codeine

8. Novocaine is derived from the 8.____
   A. coca plant B. poppy plant
   C. hemp plant D. ergot fungus

9. Nissl's granules are found in the 9.____
   A. kidney B. heart C. brain D. lung

10. The food substance which when absorbed by the body is MOST likely to increase the colloidal osmotic pressure of the blood is 10.____
    A. carbohydrates B. fats
    C. glucoses D. proteins

11. An acid ash is yielded by body oxidation of 11.___
A. meats B. citrus fruits
C. potatoes D. cream

12. A precursor of vitamin A is 12.___
A. ergosterol B. carotene
C. lysine D. pyrodoxine

13. Cells in the body which devour harmful bacteria are known as 13.___
A. anthracites B. erythrocytes
C. phagocytes D. parasites

14. At present, antibiotics are recognized to be 14.___
A. a factor in altering the natural germ balance in the body
B. ineffective in developing toxic reactions
C. ineffective in developing allergic reactions
D. most desirable in fixed antibiotic combinations

15. The study of pathogenic organisms in relation to disease is the science of 15.___
A. microbiology B. blocking therapy
C. chemotherapy D. replacement therapy

16. Atoms of an element that differ in atomic weight are called 16.___
A. molecules B. neutrons C. isotopes D. particles

17. The danger of strontium 90 lies in the fact that it 17.___
A. is absorbed and concentrated in bone tissue
B. causes tumors in smooth muscles
C. falls back and is absorbed by the soil near the explosion
D. renders the atmosphere unfit for breathing

18. Heat destroys bacteria by 18.___
A. enucleation
B. coagulating protein
C. hemolysis
D. making the cell wall permeable

19. The organ MOST commonly affected by arteriosclerosis is the 19.___
A. brain B. lung C. kidney D. heart

20. Some carbohydrates are required in a diabetic diet in order that 20.___
A. sugars may be avoided
B. fats may be oxidized
C. loss of weight may be prevented
D. intestinal putrefaction may be reduced

21. Carbohydrates are stored in the liver in the form of 21.___
A. maltose B. glycogen C. dextrose D. glucose

22. Ptyalin initiates the digestion of 22.___
A. sugars B. fats C. starches D. proteins

23. The enzyme which functions ONLY in an acid medium is 23.___
A. pepsin B. amylopsin C. ptyalin D. trypsin

24. Sulphonamides 24.___
A. prevent the growth of bacteria
B. destroy bacteria
C. attenuate bacteria
D. increase body resistance to bacteria

25. The part of the brain that is associated with memory is the 25.___
A. cerebellum B. pons varolii
C. medulla oblongata D. cerebrum

KEY (CORRECT ANSWERS)

1. C
2. D
3. A
4. D
5. D

6. A
7. A
8. A
9. C
10. D

11. A
12. B
13. C
14. A
15. A

16. C
17. A
18. B
19. C
20. B

21. B
22. C
23. A
24. A
25. D

TEST 4

DIRECTIONS: Each question or incomplete statement is followed by several suggested answers or completions. Select the one that BEST answers the question or completes the statement. *PRINT THE LETTER OF THE CORRECT ANSWER IN THE SPACE AT THE RIGHT.*

1. The compound which is NOT a constituent of normal urine is 1.___
   A. ammonia B. creatinine
   C. hippuric acid D. indican

2. A water solution of ammonia is a(n) 2.___
   A. acid B. basic salt C. base D. acid salt

3. The substances that are NOT miscible are 3.___
   A. olive oil and acetic acid
   B. glycerine and alcohol
   C. soap and water
   D. linseed oil and lime water

4. The downward pressure of the water in an enema can depend upon the 4.___
   A. speed of flow
   B. size of the tube opening
   C. quantity of fluid used
   D. the height of the surface of the water above the patient

5. A stimulant for the respiratory center is 5.___
   A. carbon dioxide B. ethyl chloride
   C. oxygen D. nitrous oxide

6. The parts of the nervous system stimulated by strychnine are the 6.___
   A. hepatic and renal nerves
   B. brain and spinal cord
   C. autonomic ganglia and sciatic nerves
   D. coronary and pulmonary nerves

7. Solutions are absorbed MORE rapidly when 7.___
   A. they are in concentrated form
   B. they are slightly diluted
   C. spread over a large surface
   D. spread over a limited area

8. The effect of below-freezing temperatures on microbes is to 8.___
   A. destroy the pathogens
   B. kill them
   C. stimulate sporification
   D. check growth and multiplication

9. Boiling an article in water for 10 minutes will destroy 9.___
   A. pathogens
   B. non-spore-forming microbes
   C. spore-forming microbes
   D. spore-forming pathogens

10. An inexpensive disinfectant is 10.___
   A. bichloride of mercury B. potassium permanganate
   C. creosote D. alcohol

11. Vitamin A is stored in the 11.___
   A. skeletal muscles B. liver
   C. thyroid D. brain

12. Swelling, heat, and redness occur in an inflamed area because the capillaries become 12.___
   A. constricted B. dilated
   C. ruptured D. fenestrated

13. Bone owes its hardness CHIEFLY to the mineral salt 13.___
   A. calcium phosphorus B. potassium iodide
   C. sodium carbonate D. stearic acid

14. The number of vertebrae of the spinal column of a human is 14.___
   A. 33 B. 42 C. 28 D. 21

15. Sebaceous glands 15.___
   A. aid digestion
   B. have ducts
   C. are attached to the muscles of the eye
   D. increase blood pressure

16. Mastoid is 16.___
   A. a woman who practices massage
   B. marasmus
   C. part of the temporal bone
   D. inflammation of the breast

17. Morphology is a study of 17.___
   A. form B. trench mouth
   C. death D. the fetus

18. The Rh factors are 18.___
   A. negative B. positive
   C. negative and positive D. none of the above

19. Fungus is a 19.___
   A. form of plant life
   B. division of a nucleus
   C. medication for inducing sleep
   D. vitamin deficiency

20. Pigmentation 20.___
   A. depends upon the hemoglobin
   B. reduces body heat
   C. protects tissues of the skin
   D. produces color

21. In respiration, 21.___
    A. expiration is slower than inspiration
    B. receptors of the skin respond
    C. the hypothalmus is expanded
    D. enzymes are rendered inert

22. The permanent teeth in human adults should number 22.___
    A. 27 B. 32 C. 26 D. 34

23. The brain 23.___
    A. is dependent upon glucose for its energy
    B. functions in the final destruction of the red blood cells
    C. appears biconcave, is elastic and pliable
    D. separates the high pressure system of the arterial tree from the lower pressure system of the venous tree

24. Taste buds are located on the tongue and 24.___
    A. on the soft palate
    B. at the Eustachian tube
    C. on posterior descending branch of the coronary
    D. in the atrium

25. Metabolism 25.___
    A. expresses the fact that nerve fibres give only one kind of reaction
    B. summarizes the activities each living cell must carry on
    C. possesses the properties of irritability and conductivity
    D. describes the membrane theory

KEY (CORRECT ANSWERS)

1. D
2. C
3. A
4. D
5. A

6. B
7. C
8. D
9. B
10. C

11. B
12. B
13. A
14. A
15. B

16. C
17. A
18. C
19. A
20. D

21. A
22. B
23. A
24. A
25. B

TEST 5

DIRECTIONS: Each question or incomplete statement is followed by several suggested answers or completions. Select the one that BEST answers the question or completes the statement. *PRINT THE LETTER OF THE CORRECT ANSWER IN THE SPACE AT THE RIGHT.*

1. The heat of the body is maintained by 1.___
   A. oxidation B. vertigo C. gravity D. hyperpnea

2. All cells 2.___
   A. exist proximal to liquid environment
   B. secrete a hormone which helps maintain the normal calcium level of the blood
   C. differ in origin and function
   D. are cone-shaped

3. The heart rate 3.___
   A. varies in individuals
   B. increases from birth to old age
   C. increases during first hours of sleep
   D. decreases in hemorrhage

4. A neuron consists of 4.___
   A. fluid in the semicircular canals
   B. conjugated protein which yields globin and heme
   C. a cell body and processes
   D. a band of spectrum colors ranging from red to violet

5. The process of swallowing is called 5.___
   A. delactation B. diastasis
   C. deglutition D. emission

6. Histology 6.___
   A. dissolves essential constituents in water
   B. connects arterial and venous circulation
   C. describes microscopic structure
   D. reduces diseased structures

7. When water is added to dry mustard, the reaction is 7.___
   A. polymerization B. hydrolysis
   C. dehydration D. neutralization

8. The efficacy of saline cathartics depends upon the 8.___
   A. selective action
   B. osmotic pressure
   C. relaxation of smooth muscle
   D. retarding of peristalsis

9. The chemical which stimulates the respiratory center is 9.___
   A. oxygen B. carbon dioxide
   C. calcium D. nitrogen

10. Carbon dioxide and oxygen are exchanged in the air sacs by 10.___
A. infusion B. diffusion
C. reaction D. filtration

11. The absorption of water through the intestinal wall is by 11.___
A. filtration B. osmosis
C. infiltration D. fusion

12. Oils and water do not mix readily because of the difference in 12.___
A. heat of fusion B. surface tension
C. heat of sublimation D. freezing point

13. The lowering of the head when a person feels faint will increase the blood supply to the head by 13.___
A. suction B. gravity
C. siphonage D. centripetal force

14. The ventricles of the heart act like a 14.___
A. lever B. pump C. siphon D. barometer

15. A rubber hot water bottle transfers heat to the skin CHIEFLY by 15.___
A. conduction B. convection
C. radiation D. oxidation

16. A clinical thermometer is a(n) 16.___
A. thermograph B. maximum thermometer
C. minimum thermometer D. absolute thermometer

17. To increase the solubility of boric acid powder in water, 17.___
A. increase the temperature of the water
B. add boric powder rapidly
C. decrease the area of contact with water
D. supersaturate the water

18. The CHIEF component of Monel metal equipment is 18.___
A. nickel B. copper C. chromium D. silicon

19. The contractility of the heart CANNOT be maintained in the absence of 19.___
A. nitrogen B. hydrogen C. sodium D. vitamin D

20. Prolonged diarrhea can result in acidosis, due to loss of 20.___
A. salts B. glucose
C. body heat D. carbon dioxide

21. The fulcrum of an extremity is at the 21.___
A. joint B. bone C. cartilage D. muscle

22. Measurements of aqueous solutions are made from the bottom of the meniscus because water is ____ glass. 22.___
A. adhesive toward B. absorbed by
C. diffused through D. cohesive toward

23. Chemical heating bottles which employ the use of sodium salts produce heat by 23.___
   A. crystallization B. ionization
   C. fermentation D. hydrogenation

24. A rubber sheet is uncomfortable because rubber 24.___
   A. promotes evaporation
   B. absorbs perspiration
   C. is a poor conductor of heat
   D. is porous

25. The solution which should be administered through a glass drinking tube is 25.___
   A. sodium borate B. magnesium sulfate
   C. ferrous sulfate D. calcium carbonate

KEY (CORRECT ANSWERS)

1. A
2. A
3. A
4. C
5. C

6. C
7. B
8. B
9. B
10. B

11. B
12. B
13. B
14. B
15. A

16. B
17. A
18. A
19. C
20. A

21. A
22. A
23. A
24. C
25. C

TEST 6

DIRECTIONS: Each question or incomplete statement is followed by several suggested answers or completions. Select the one that BEST answers the question or completes the statement. *PRINT THE LETTER OF THE CORRECT ANSWER IN THE SPACE AT THE RIGHT.*

1. A forceps is a _____ lever. 1.___
   A. first class B. second class
   C. third class D. bent

2. Hydrogen peroxide disinfects by 2.___
   A. rupturing the bacterial cell
   B. precipitating protein
   C. bacteriostasis
   D. liberating nascent oxygen

3. Hot drinks increase body heat CHIEFLY by 3.___
   A. convection B. radiation
   C. evaporation D. conduction

4. A GOOD solvent for removing adhesive markings from the skin is 4.___
   A. rubbing alcohol B. liquor antisepticus
   C. zephiran D. benzine

5. If a thermometer is broken in the mouth, the mercury will NOT be injurious because the mercury 5.___
   A. has been treated to prevent chemical change
   B. will vaporize rapidly
   C. absorbs heat from the mucous membranes
   D. is in the pure inert state

6. The effectiveness of oral Penicillin is limited due to the 6.___
   A. need for greater purification
   B. formation of an insoluble compound
   C. irregular absorption
   D. irritation of the mucous membrane

7. The action by which dentrifices clean the teeth is CHIEFLY 7.___
   A. chemical B. bacteriological
   C. mechanical D. thermal

8. A difference between gamma globulin and polio vaccine is gamma globulin contains 8.___
   A. attenuated organisms B. antibodies
   C. dead virus D. antigens

9. Pulverizing a pill before administration will increase the speed of action by 9.___
   A. changing its chemical composition
   B. decreasing its solubility

C. decreasing the alkalinity of the stomach
D. increasing the surface area of contact

10. The virus in polio vaccine is 10.___
A. virulent B. inactivated
C. suspended D. emulsified

11. Antibiotics may produce 11.___
A. imbalance in normal bacterial flora
B. injury to blood forming organs
C. inhibition of motility of the stomach
D. injury to red blood cells

12. The PRINCIPAL organic constituent of perspiration is 12.___
A. stearic acid B. lachrymal
C. urea D. oxalic acid

13. The bactericidal action of perspiration is dependent upon its 13.___
A. turbidity B. viscosity
C. pH D. color

14. A substance which is NOT found in normal urine is 14.___
A. urea B. chloride C. creatinine D. acetone

15. Many of the bacteria which enter the stomach with food are either inhibited or destroyed by the 15.___
A. high concentration of hydrogen ions
B. mucin and salts
C. gastric lipase
D. enterogastrone

16. The tendon of Achilles is attached to the 16.___
A. scapula B. femur C. calcaneus D. clavicle

17. The hyoid is the 17.___
A. u-shaped bone in the neck between the mandible and upper part of the larynx
B. first of the upper seven vertebra
C. breast bone
D. knee cap

18. The ulna is located at or near the 18.___
A. second cervical vertebra
B. elbow
C. arch into which the lower teeth are set
D. knee cap

19. To test urine for sugar content, the proportion of urine to Fehling's solution should be ____ cc. to 1 _____. 19.___
A. 3; tablespoon B. 1; teaspoon
C. 3; teaspoon D. 1; tablespoon

20. The substance which is NOT found in vitamin B complex is 20.___
A. nicotinic acid B. thiamine
C. prothrombin D. riboflavin

21. The fat soluble vitamins are 21.____
    A. A, D, E, C B. vitamin B complex
    C. A, D, E, K D. A, C, E, K

22. The contraction of the heart muscle is caused by 22.____
    A. the systolic and diastolic (contraction and relaxation) periods
    B. many toxins accumulated in the blood by exercise
    C. the proper functioning of other organs in the body
    D. its own nerve tissue stimulated by chemical action of salts in the blood

23. The difference between the systolic and diastolic blood pressure is known as pulse pressure which should equal _____ millimeters mercuric pressure. 23.____
    A. 80 B. 60 C. 40 D. 20

24. The normal sugar content of the blood is APPROXIMATELY one part sugar to 24.____
    A. one thousand parts blood
    B. five thousand parts blood
    C. ten thousand parts blood
    D. none of the above

25. The nucleus of body cells contains chromatin. This substance is concerned with 25.____
    A. the process of cell division by which new cells develop through the process of mitosis
    B. chemical changes in foods
    C. the continued health status of cells
    D. the physical basis of heredity

KEY (CORRECT ANSWERS)

1. C
2. D
3. D
4. D
5. D

6. C
7. C
8. B
9. D
10. C

11. A
12. C
13. C
14. D
15. A

16. C
17. A
18. B
19. B
20. D

21. D
22. D
23. D
24. B
25. D

TEST 7

DIRECTIONS: Each question or incomplete statement is followed by several suggested answers or completions. Select the one that BEST answers the question or completes the statement. *PRINT THE LETTER OF THE CORRECT ANSWER IN THE SPACE AT THE RIGHT.*

1. Salts which affect the acidity or alkalinity of the protoplasm are said to have a(n) _____ effect. 1.____
   A. osmotic B. buffer
   C. condensation D. reduction

2. The vitamin destroyed by heat in the presence of oxygen is 2.____
   A. G B. C C. A D. B

3. It is difficult to destroy tubercle bacilli in the human body because of the 3.____
   A. ability of the bacilli to form spores
   B. resistance of the bacilli
   C. rapid multiplication of the bacilli
   D. bacilli in body locale

4. In diseases of the liver, the diet should be 4.____
   A. *high* in protein and *low* in carbohydrates
   B. *high* in fat and carbohydrates
   C. *low* in protein and fat and *high* in carbohydrates
   D. *high* in carbohydrates and *low* in protein

5. When sodium fluoride is combined with calcium, it USUALLY _____ formation. 5.____
   A. retards acid B. speeds acid
   C. retards alkali D. speeds alkali

6. The thermatron is used to take temperature of the 6.____
   A. incubator B. vaporizer
   C. sterilizer D. blood donor

7. The destruction of red blood cells by sporozoites frees toxins which produce 7.____
   A. erythroblastosis fetalis B. malarial syndromes
   C. pernicious anemia D. primary anemia

8. The drug which has been produced without using molds is 8.____
   A. streptomycin B. chloromycetin
   C. aureomycin D. penicillin

9. A shielded concentrated source for deep therapy is 9.____
   A. Cobalt 60 B. Radium C. Polonium D. Plutonium

10. For close work, the foot-candle illumination should be AT LEAST 10.____
   A. 30 B. 10 C. 15 D. 25

11. Louis Pasteur is known for his work on 11.___
A. tuberculosis B. smallpox
C. puerperal fever D. rabies prevention

12. Ultraviolet rays are enclosed in quartz tubes because the rays can be 12.___
A. uncontrolled B. measured
C. filtered D. concentrated

13. Carbohydrate metabolism is GREATLY influenced by the following vitamin: 13.___
A. thiamin B. vitamin E
C. ascorbic acid D. vitamin A

14. Vitamin C deficiency causes 14.___
A. weakened capillary walls
B. nightblindness
C. an increase in ear infections
D. photophobia

15. Plasma is about _____ protein. 15.___
A. 7% B. 80% C. 20% D. 75%

16. Lysol and creolin are used in solutions for hands in the strength of _____ percent. 16.___
A. $\frac{1}{4}$ to $\frac{1}{2}$ B. 1 to 2 C. 3 to 4 D. 5 to 10

17. For terminal disinfection of thermometers, soak them in a covered dish containing 70% alcohol for _____ hour(s). 17.___
A. one half B. three C. six D. twelve

18. The element essential in the biological oxidation of sugar is 18.___
A. phosphorus B. sodium
C. potassium D. iron

19. The addition of sodium bicarbonate in cooking speeds up the destruction of vitamin 19.___
A. B B. D C. A D. C

20. Lymph is found in all of the following places EXCEPT 20.___
A. pleural cavity B. bursae
C. cerebrospinal fluid D. in the diaphysis

21. The application of sodium fluoride solution to the teeth will 21.___
A. not prevent dental caries
B. cause more harm than benefit
C. not halt tooth decay once it has started
D. discolor the enamel

22. The microorganism which has more than one cell is 22.___
A. yeast B. mold
C. diatom D. malaria plasmodium

23. Red blood cells 23.____
A. fight infection
B. give color to the blood
C. carry food and oxygen
D. discard carbon dioxide

24. Antitoxins are 24.____
A. attenuated organisms
B. dead organisms
C. sera containing antibodies
D. bacillary toxins

25. Fraternal twins come from 25.____
A. the union of one female and one male cell
B. two separate female cells and two separate male cells
C. one female cell and two male cells
D. two female cells and one male cell

KEY (CORRECT ANSWERS)

1. B
2. B
3. D
4. A
5. A

6. D
7. B
8. B
9. A
10. C

11. D
12. C
13. C
14. A
15. A

16. B
17. D
18. A
19. A
20. D

21. C
22. B
23. C
24. C
25. B

COMMON DIAGNOSTIC NORMS

CONTENTS

	Page
1. Respiration	1
2. Pulse-Rate	1
3. Blood Pressure	1
4. Blood Metabolism	1
5. Blood	1
6. Urine	2
7. Spinal Fluid	3
8. Snellen Chart Fractions	4

COMMON DIAGNOSTIC NORMS

1. RESPIRATION: From 16-20 per minute.

2. PULSE-RATE: Men, about 72 per minute.
   Women, about 80 per minute.

3. BLOOD PRESSURE: Men, 110-135 (Systolic) 70- 85 (Diastolic) Women: 95-125 (Systolic) 65- 70 (Diastolic)

4. BASAL METABOLISM: Represents the body energy expended to maintain respiration, circulation, etc. Normal rate ranges from plus 10 to minus 10.

5. BLOOD:
   a. Red Blood (Erythrocyte) Count -
      Male Adult - 5,000,000 per cu. mm.
      Female Adult - 4,500,000 per cu. mm.

      (Increased in polycythemia vera, poisoning by carbon monoxide, in chronic pulmonary artery sclerosis, and in concentration of blood by sweating, vomiting or diarrhea).

      (Decreased in pernicious anemia, secondary anemia, and hypochromic anemia).

   b. White Blood (Leukocyte) Count -
      6,000 to 8,000 per cu. mm.

      (Increased with muscular exercise, acute infections, intestinal obstruction, coronary thrombosis, leukemias).

      (Decreased due to injury to source of blood formation and interference in delivery of cells to blood stream, typhoid, pernicious anemia, arsenic and benzol poisoning).

      The total leukocyte group is made up of a number of diverse varieties of white blood cells. Not only the total leukocyte count, but also the relative count of the diverse varieties, is an important aid to diagnosis. In normal blood, from:

      70-72% of the leukocytes are "polymorphonuclear neutrophils."
      2-4% of the leukocytes are "polymorphonuclear eosinophils."
      0.5% of the leukocytes are "basophils."
      20-25% of the leukocytes are "lymphocytes."
      2-6% of the leukocytes are "monocytes."

   c. Blood Platelet (Thrombocyte) Count -
      250,000 per cu. mm. Blood platelets are important in blood coagulation.

   d. Hemoglobin Content -
      May normally vary from 85% - 100%. A 100% hemoglobin content is equivalent to the presence of 15.6 grams of hemoglobin in 100 c.c. of blood.

   e. Color Index -
      Represents the relative amount of hemoglobin contained in a red blood corpuscle compared with that of a normal individual of the patient's age and sex.

      The normal is 1. To determine the color index, the percentage of hemoglobin is divided by the ratio of red cells in the patient's blood to a norm of 5,000,000. Thus, a hemoglobin content of 60% and a red-cell count of 4,000,000 (80% of 5,000,000) produces an abnormal color index of .75.

f. Sedimentation Rate -

Represents the measurement of the speed with which red cells settle toward the bottom of a containing vessel. The rate is expressed in millimeters per hour, and indicates the total sedimentation of red blood cells at the end of 60 minutes.

Average rate:	4-7 mm. in 1 hour
Slightly abnormal rate:	8-15 mm. in 1 hour
Moderately abnormal rate:	16-40 mm. in 1 hour
Considerably abnormal rate:	41-80 mm. in 1 hour

(The sedimentation rate is above normal in patients with chronic infections, or in whom there is a disease process involving destruction of tissue, such as coronary thrombosis, etc.)

g. Blood Sugar -

90-120 mg. per 100 c.c. (Normal)
In mild diabetics: 150-300 mg. per 100 c.c.
In severe diabetics: 300-1200 mg. per 100 c.c.

h. Blood Lead -

0.1 mg. or less in 100 c.c. (Normal). Greatly increased in lead poisoning.

i. Non-Protein Nitrogen -

Since the function of the kidneys is to remove from the blood certain of the waste products of cellular activity, any degree of accumulation of these waste products in the blood is a measure of renal malfunction. For testing purposes, the substances chosen for measurement are the nitrogen - containing products of protein combustion, their amounts being estimated in terms of the nitrogen they contain. These substances are urea, uric acid and creatinine, the sum-total of which, in addition to any traces of other waste products, being designated as total non-protein nitrogen (NPN).

The normal limits of NPN in 100 c.c. of blood range from 25-40 mg. Of this total, Urea Nitrogen normally constitutes 12-15 mg.; Uric Acid 2-4 mg.; and creatinine 1-2 mg.

6. URINE:

a. Urine - Lead -

0.08 mg. per liter of urine. (Normal).
(Increased in lead poisoning).

b. Sugar -

From none to a faint trace. (Normal).
From 0.5% upwards. (Abnormal).
(Increased in diabetes mellitus).

c. Urea -

Normal excretion ranges from 15-40 grams in 24 hours.
(Increased in fever and toxic states).

d. Uric Acid -

Normal excretion is variable.
(Increased in leukemia, and gout).

e. Albumin-

Normal renal cells allow a trace of albumin to pass into the urine, but this trace is so minute that it cannot be detected by ordinary tests.

f. Casts -

In some abnormal conditions the kidney tubules become lined with substances which harden and form a mould or "cast" inside the tubes. These are later washed out by the urine, and may be detected microscopically. They are named either from the substance composing them, or from their appearance. Thus there are pus casts; epithelial casts from the walls of the tubes; hyaline casts, formed from coagulable elements of the blood, etc.

g. Pus Cells -

These are found in the urine in cases of nephritis or other inflammatory conditions of the urinary tract.

h. Epithelial Cells-

These are always present in the urine. Their number is greatly multiplied, however, in inflammatory conditions of the urinary tract.

i. Specific Gravity-

This is the ratio between the weight of a given volume of urine to that of the same volume of water. A normal reading ranges from 1.015 to 1.025. A high specific gravity usually occurs in diabetes mellitus. A low specific gravity is associated with a polyuria.

7. SPINAL FLUID:

a. Spinal Fluid Pressure (Manometric Reading)-

100-200 mm. of water or 7-15 mm. of mercury. (Normal).

(Increased in cerebral edema, cerebral hemorrhage, meningitis, certain brain tumors, or if there is some process blocking the fluid circulation in the spinal column, - such as a tumor or herniated nucleus pulposus impinging on the spinal canal).

b. Quickenstedt's Sign-

When the veins in the neck are compressed on one or both sides, there is a rapid rise in the pressure of the cerebrospinal fluid of healthy persons, and this rise quickly disappears when pressure is removed from the neck. But when there is a block of the vertebral canal, the pressure of the cerebrospinal fluid is little or not at all affected by this maneuver.

c. Cerebrospinal Sugar-

50-60 mg. per 100 c.c. of spinal fluid. (Normal).

(Increased in epidemic encephalitis, diabetes mellitus, and increased intracranial pressure).

(Decreased in purulent and tuberculous meningitis).

d. Cerebrospinal Protein-

15-40 mg. per 100 c.c. of spinal fluid. (Normal).

(Increased in suppurative meningitis, epileptic seizures, cerebrospinal syphilis, anterior poliomyelitis, brain abscess, and brain tumor).

e. Colloidal Gold Test-

This test is made to determine the presence of cerebrospinal protein.

f. Cerebrospinal Cell Count-

0-10 lymphocytes per cu. mm. (Normal).

g. Cerebrospinal Globulin-

Normally negative. It is positive in various types of meningitis, various types of syphilis of the central nervous system, in poliomyelitis, in brain tumor and in intracranial hemorrhage.

8. SNELLEN CHART FRACTIONS AS SCHEDULE LOSS DETERMINANTS:

a. Visual acuity is expressed by a Snell Fraction, where the numerator represents the distance, in feet, between the subject and the test chart, and the denominator represents the distance, in feet, at which a normal eye could read a type size which the abnormal eye can read only at 20 feet.

b. Thus, 20/20 means that an individual placed 20 feet from the test chart clearly sees the size of type that one with normal vision should see at that distance.

c. 20/60 means that an individual placed 20 feet from the test chart can read only a type-size, at a distance of 20 feet, which one of normal vision could read at 60 feet.

d. Reduction of a Snellen Fraction to its simplest form roughly indicates the amount of vision remaining in an eye. Thus, a visual acuity of 20/60 corrected, implies a useful vision of 1/3 or 33 1/3%, and a visual loss of 2/3 or 66 2/3% of the eye.

Similarly:

Visual Acuity (Corrected)	Percentage Loss of Use of Eye
20/20	No loss
20/25	20%
20/30	33 1/3%
20/40	50%
20/50	60%
20/60	66 2/3%
20/70	70% (app.)
20/80	75%
20/100	100% (Since loss of 80% or more constitutes industrial blindness)

BASIC FUNDAMENTALS OF MEDICATION ADMINISTRATION

CONTENTS

	Page
I. GUIDELINES FOR MEDICATION ADMINISTRATION	1
A. General	1
B. Unit Dose	3
II. MEDICATION ADMINISTRATION RECORD	4
III. DROPS	7
A. Ear	7
B. Eye	8
C. Nose	9
IV. GASTRIC TUBES	10
V. HEPARIN LOCKS	11
VI. INJECTIONS	12
A. General	12
B. Intramuscular	14
1. Z-Tract	15
C. Intradermal	15
D. Intravenous Piggyback	16
E. Subcutaneous	18
1. Insulin	19
VII. ORAL MEDICATIONS	19
A. Tablets, Pills, or Capsules	20
B. Powders	20
C. Liquids	20
VIII. SUPPOSITORIES	21
A. Rectal	21
B. Urethral	22
C. Vaginal	23

BASIC FUNDAMENTALS OF MEDICATION ADMINISTRATION

I. *GUIDELINES FOR MEDICATION ADMINISTRATION*

A. General

PURPOSE

To administer the right medication, in the right dose, by the right route, to the right patient, at the right time

PROCEDURE	SPECIAL CONSIDERATIONS
• Transcribe medication and treatment orders from doctor's orders to • Medication and Treatment Cards • Nursing Care Plan • Medication Administration Record (MAR)	Follow local policy.
• Check ALL Medication and Treatment Cards against Nursing Care Plan at the beginning of each shift.	
• Return cards to medication and treatment board, placing each card in space corresponding to hour when medication is due.	
• Clean working area.	
• Wash your hands.	
• Obtain supplies and equipment such as tongue blades, paper cups, pitcher of water, medication tray or cart, and stethoscope.	
• Separate cards into • oral medications • injections • treatments	
• Arrange cards in sequence similar to placement of patients on ward.	Keep cards for same patient together.
• Turn cards face down, turn top card up, and read information on card.	
• Locate medication and compare label on medication with name of medication and dosage on card.	FIRST MEDICATION CHECK.

GUIDELINES FOR MEDICATION ADMINISTRATION, GENERAL (cont)

PROCEDURE	SPECIAL CONSIDERATIONS
• Remove medication container and compare label on container with name of medication and dosage on card.	SECOND CHECK.
• Pour required dosage and compare label on container with card for name of medication and dosage.	THIRD CHECK.
• Place medication and card on tray or cart.	NEVER leave medication cart or tray unattended.
• Continue with remaining cards in same manner.	
• Lock medication cabinet before leaving the area.	
• Administer only medications that you personally prepared.	NEVER allow others to administer medication that you prepared.
• Check name on bed tag with name on card.	FIRST ID CHECK.
• Compare name on card with patient's ID band.	SECOND CHECK.
• Ask patient: "What is your name?" Be sure response is accurate.	THIRD CHECK.
• Administer medication ONLY if all 3 checks agree.	
• Place card face down on one side of tray.	
• Continue to administer medications until all are given.	
• Reset tray or cart for next use.	
• Take cards to desk.	
• Record medications, time and date given, and your initials on MAR using cards as guide.	
• Replace cards on board at next hour due.	

B. *Unit Dose*

PURPOSE

To administer single-dose medication in ready-to-use form

PROCEDURE	SPECIAL CONSIDERATIONS
• See "Guidelines for Medication Administration, General."	
• Get stocked medication cart from storage area.	Cart is stocked by pharmacy personnel.
• Unlock cart.	
• Wheel medication cart to bedside, check MAR, and identify patient.	Follow local policy.
• Open cassette drawer. • Read MAR. • Select medication from cassette drawer.	
• Check medication against MAR for date, dosage, and route.	
• Administer medication and record immediately on MAR. • Remain with patient until medication has been taken. • Replace drawer in correct space in cassette.	
• Dispose of litter, syringe, and needle before moving to next patient. • Break off tip of needle and syringe, and dispose in dirty needle box. • Place glass unit dose liquid container in bag for return to pharmacy.	
• Lock cart and return to storage area.	

II. MEDICATION ADMINISTRATION RECORD (MAR)

PURPOSE

To maintain a permanent record of medication administered

PROCEDURE	SPECIAL CONSIDERATIONS
• Stamp MAR with Addressograph as shown in figure 6-1 on the following page.	
• Enter ward number at bottom right of form; record month and year in space provided at the top.	Make all entries in black ink.
• Transcribe scheduled medications from doctor's orders to front of form.	
• Enter order date, medication dosage, frequency, and route of administration.	
• Complete "Hours" column to indicate scheduled hours for administration starting with earliest military time after 2400 hours.	
• Complete "Dates Given" blocks at top of form. • Enter month and dates for a 7-day period, starting with first day medication is given.	
• Cancel vacant spaces with an "X."	
• Draw a heavy line across page under last entry and enter next medication directly below.	Do not skip a space.
• When medication has been given, enter your initials in column corresponding to date and hour of administration.	
• Place an "*" in column if the medication was not given and state reason on Nursing Notes.	
• Place an "L" under date and opposite hour patient is on liberty.	Follow local policy.
• When medication is stopped, bracket remaining spaces for that day; write "STOPPED," enter date and initials.	Applies to scheduled drugs, PRN, and variable dose medications.
• Complete "Initial Code" section.	

NAVMED 6550/8 (REV. 4-74) S/N 0105-LF-216-5581

MEDICAL RECORD

MEDICATION ADMINISTRATION RECORD

SCHEDULED DRUGS

MONTH June 1979 DATES GIVEN

ORDER DATE	MEDICATION-DOSAGE-FREQUENCY ROUTE OF ADMINISTRATION	HOURS	6/19/79	6/20	6/21	6/22	6/23	6/24	6/25
6/19/79	Digoxin 0.25mg PO QD	0800	JLD	*	JLD	JLD	JLD		
	APICAL PULSE →		72	58	64	68	70		
6/19/79	INDERAL 40mg PO Q6H	0600	X	JEP	JEP	Stopped 6/22/79 JLD			
		1200	X	JLD	JLD				
		1800	JMW	JMW	JMW				
		2400	JMW	JEP	JEP				
6/19/79	Regular Insulin Sliding Scale								
	Glucose 4+ Reg. Insulin 10U sc	0700	JLD 5U	X	JLD 10U	X	JLD 10U		
	Glucose 3+ Reg. Insulin 7U sc	1100	X	X	X	RAB 7U	X		
	Glucose 2+ Reg Insulin 5U sc	1600	JMW 5U	JMW 7U	X	X	X		
	Glucose 1+ Reg. Insulin 0U sc	2100	X	X	X	X	X		
6/19/79	MAALOX 15ml PO Q1H	0800-1500	JLD	JLD	JLD	RAB	JLD		
		1600-2300	JMW	JMW	JMW	JMW	JMW		
		2400-0700	JEP	JEP	JEP	JEP	JEP		
6/20/79	DECADRON (Decreasing dose)	0200	X	RAB 4mg	RAB 3mg	RAB 2mg	RAB 1mg		
	4mg PO Q4H x 12hrs	0600	X	RAB 4mg	RAB 3mg	RAB 2mg	RAB 1mg		
	3mg PO Q4H x 24 hrs	1000	X	RAB 4mg	RAB 3mg	RAB 2mg	RAB 1mg		
	2mg PO Q4H x 24 hrs	1400	X	RAB 3mg	SEB 2mg	SEB 1mg	SEB 0.5mg		
	1mg PO Q4H x 24 hrs	1800	X	SEB 3mg	SEB 2mg	SEB 1mg	SEB 0.5mg		
	0.5mg PO Q4H x 12 hrs	2200	X	SEB 3mg	SEB 2mg	SEB 1mg	SEB 0.5mg		
	then DC								

INITIAL CODE

INITIAL	FULL SIGNATURE & TITLE	INITIAL	FULL SIGNATURE & TITLE	INITIAL	FULL SIGNATURE & TITLE
JLD	John L. Dace LT NC USN				
JMW	Jane M. White LT NC USN				
SEB	Stanley E Baker HM3 USN				
RAB	Ronald A Barnes HN USN				
JEP	Joan E Pierce CDR NC USN				
CFR	Charles F Roberts HM3 USN				

ADDRESSOGRAPH PLATE

J-999999 00-123-45-6789
24JAN79 PROT M E9
22MAY36 MMCM/USN/ACT
DOE, JOHN E. AAA

WARD NO. T8

Injection Site Code

1 = Left Buttock
2 = Right Buttock
3 = Left Deltoid
4 = Right Deltoid
5 = Left Leg
6 = Right Leg
7 = Left Arm
8 = Right Arm
9 = Abdomen

SINGLE DOSE, PRE-OP PRN & VARIABLE DOSE ORDERS SEE REVERSE

Figure 1. Sample Entries on Medication Administration Record (Front).

MEDICATION ADMINISTRATION RECORD (cont)

PROCEDURE

SPECIAL CONSIDERATIONS

• Transcribe single-order medication, dosage, route of administration, and date and time to be given on back of form. See figure 2 on the following page.

• After administering medication, initial appropriate block.

• Transcribe each preoperative (PREOP) medication dosage, and route of administration on succeeding lines.

A bracket may be used to show that all PREOP medications are to be given on the same date and time.

• Enter your initials after administering medications.

• Transcribe PRN and variable dose medications from doctor's orders to back of form (fig. 2).

• Enter order date, medication, dosage, frequency, route, and reason for medication.

For variable dose medications, the dosage need not be the same for each entry.

• Enter date, time, dose, and your initials after administering medication.

NOTE: Some medication orders require modification of basic transcription and charting techniques (fig. 1). These include:

- increasing or decreasing dose medications
- medications requiring apical pulse assessment before administration
- medications administered every other day
- medications such as insulin administered per sliding scale

MEDICATION ADMINISTRATION RECORD (Back) S/N 0105-LF-216-5581

SINGLE ORDERS – PRE-OPERATIVE

MEDICATION-DOSAGE ROUTE OF ADMINISTRATION	GIVEN			MEDICATION-DOSAGE ROUTE OF ADMINISTRATION	GIVEN		
	DATE	TIME	INITIAL		DATE	TIME	INITIAL
Nitroglycerine 0.4 mg Subling.	6/19/79	1200	JLD				
Demerol 100 mg IM } Pre op	6/24/79	0700	JLD				
Nembutal 100 mg IM }	6/24/79	0700	JLD				

PRN AND VARIABLE DOSE MEDICATIONS

ORDER DATE	MEDICATION-DOSAGE FREQUENCY ROUTE OF ADMINISTRATION		DOSES GIVEN
6/22/79	Diazepam 5 mg	DATE	6/22
	PO PRN restlessness	TIME	1800
		DOSE	5 mg
		INIT.	SEB
		DATE	
		TIME	
		DOSE	
		INIT.	

Figure 2. Sample Entries on Medication Administration Record (Back).

III. DROPS

A. Ear

PURPOSE

To instill medication into the auditory canal

PROCEDURE

- See "Guidelines for Medication Administration, General."
- Position patient on side with affected ear upward.
- Clean external auditory canal gently with cotton applicators.
- Straighten auditory canal by gently pulling lobe upward and backward.

SPECIAL CONSIDERATIONS

Patients should have their own properly labeled medication and it should be at room temperature.

Avoid traumatizing when dry-wiping ear canal.

DROPS, EAR (cont)

PROCEDURE

- Instill prescribed number of drops holding dropper nearly horizontally.
- Place cotton loosely in external auditory canal (if ordered).
- Instruct patient to remain in position with treated ear upward for about 5 minutes.

SPECIAL CONSIDERATIONS

Support head as needed. Allow medication to fall to side of canal.

SUPPLIES AND EQUIPMENT

Applicators, cotton tipped

Cotton balls

B. *Eye* (Ointment Included)

PURPOSE

To apply medication to eye tissue

PROCEDURE

- See "Guidelines for Medication Administration."
- Verify eye to be medicated.
- Tilt patient's head backward and sideways so solution will run away from tear duct.
- Clean eye gently with cotton ball.
- Retract lower lid.
- Instruct patient to look upward.
- Drop medication onto lower lid as shown in figure 3.

SPECIAL CONSIDERATIONS

If both drops and ointment are ordered, instill drops before applying ointment.
Patients should have their own properly labeled medication.

Some solutions are toxic if absorbed through the nose or pharynx.

Do not permit dropper or tip of ointment tube to touch the eye. Avoid contaminating medicine container.

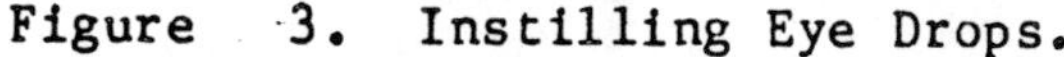

Figure 3. Instilling Eye Drops.

DROPS, EYE (cont)

PROCEDURE

• Apply ointment onto conjunctiva of lower lid as illustrated in figure 4.

• Place dropper in bottle or put cap on ointment tube.

• Instruct patient to close eye.

• Wipe excess medication from inner to outer eye with sterile 2x2s then discard.

SPECIAL CONSIDERATIONS

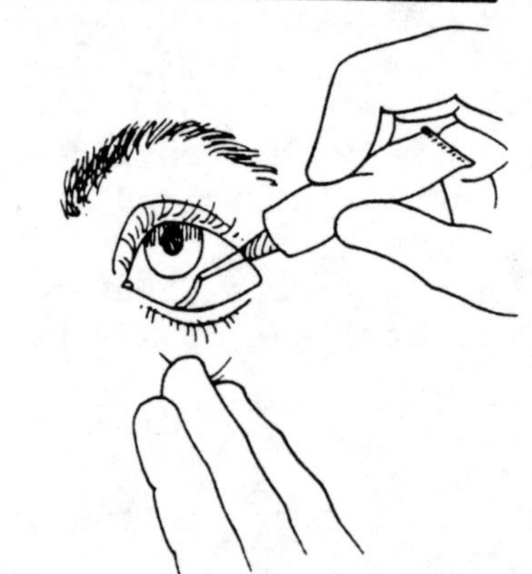

Figure 4. Instilling Eye Ointment.

SUPPLIES AND EQUIPMENT

Cotton balls

Sterile gauze 2x2s

C. *Nose*

PURPOSE

To instill medication into the nose

PROCEDURE

• See "Guidelines for Medication Administration."

• Tilt patient's head backwards.

• Fill dropper with medication.

• Instill prescribed dosage into nostril as shown in figure 5.

• Place tissues within easy reach.

• Keep patient in position for about 2 minutes.

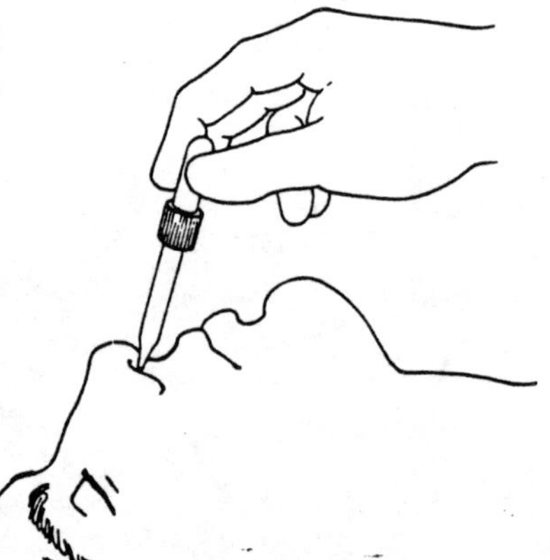

Figure 5. Instilling Nose Drops.

SPECIAL CONSIDERATIONS

Patients should have their own properly labeled medication.

Do not permit medication to touch rubber bulb of dropper.

Avoid touching nostril with tip of dropper.

IV. GASTRIC TUBES

PURPOSE

To administer medications into the stomach through a tube

PROCEDURE	SPECIAL CONSIDERATIONS
• See "Guidelines for Medication Administration, General."	
• Crush all tablets and add 30 ml tap water.	
• Assemble equipment and take to bedside.	
• Elevate head of bed unless contraindicated.	Decreases risk of aspiration and regurgitation.
• Expose feeding tube.	
• Place protective pad under tubes.	
• Check stomach tube for correct placement. • Aspirate for gastric contents. • Listen with stethoscope for air entering stomach as 5 to 10 cc of air is injected into tube.	Notify physician if tube is not placed properly.
• Attach irrigating syringe to tube with plunger removed.	
• Instill medication into irrigating syringe.	
• Follow medication with 30 ml water and allow to flow by gravity.	Ensures patient receives all medication.
• Clamp tube and cover end for 20 to 30 minutes unless contraindicated.	Allows medicine to be absorbed.
• Reattach tube to suction if indicated.	
• Rinse and clean syringe with tap water.	
• Return syringe to bedside storage.	
• Record amount of water instilled on I&O worksheet.	
• Record medication administered on MAR.	

GASTRIC TUBES (cont)

SUPPLIES AND EQUIPMENT

Clamp
Emesis basin
Gauze sponges 4x4
Irrigating syringe, 60 ml
Protective pad
Rubber band
Sterile dressing (if ordered)
Stethoscope
Tap water

V. *HEPARIN LOCKS*

PURPOSE

To administer medications through a heparin lock

PROCEDURE	SPECIAL CONSIDERATIONS
• See "Guidelines for Medication Administration, General."	
• Assemble IV piggyback (IVPB) medication and IV administration set; attach small gauge needle to end of tubing.	
• Fill two 2 1/2 ml syringes with 2 ml normal saline.	
• Withdraw 0.9 ml normal saline and 0.1 ml heparin 1:1000 into a TB syringe.	
• Take equipment to bedside.	
• Determine patency of heparin lock. • Attach first 2 1/2 ml syringe with saline. • Aspirate and observe for blood return. • If no blood returns, check for infiltration by slowly injecting small amount of normal saline. • If infiltrated, remove heparin lock and insert new one.	
• Flush lock with 2 ml normal saline to flush out heparin.	Incompatibilities may exist resulting in a precipitate.
• Attach IVPB medication infusion set to heparin lock.	
• Administer medication.	
• Flush lock with second syringe of normal saline.	

HEPARIN LOCKS (cont)

PROCEDURE	SPECIAL CONSIDERATIONS
• Flush lock with heparin solution.	
• Record medication given on MAR.	

SUPPLIES AND EQUIPMENT

Alcohol sponges	IV administration set	Syringes, 2 1/2 ml (2), TB (1)
Heparin 1:1000	IVPB infusion set	
	Needle, 23 ga	

VI. *INJECTIONS*

A. *General*

In this section, intramuscular, intradermal, and subcutaneous injections are outlined. Many of the steps are the same for all three methods of injection. Therefore, follow the basic procedure listed below and refer to the specific procedure for special details and equipment.

PROCEDURE	SPECIAL CONSIDERATIONS
• See "Guidelines for Medication Administration, General."	
• Assemble equipment in preparation area. • Remove syringe from sterile pack. • Loosen the plunger by withdrawing once or twice. • Assemble syringe and needle. . Tighten needle.	See equipment list of specific procedure.
• Score ampule with file if not prescored.	Prescored ampules are usually indicated by colored ring.
• Clean ampule or vial with antiseptic sponge and break away top of ampule.	
• Discard ampule top and sponge.	
• Remove needle guard and place on counter for reuse.	
• Draw enough air into syringe to equal in volume the dose of medication ordered.	Does not apply to ampules.

INJECTIONS, GENERAL (cont)

PROCEDURE

- Insert needle into medication using aseptic technique. See figure 6.

- Withdraw slightly more medication than required dose.

- Remove needle from ampule or vial.

- Hold syringe and needle vertically.
  - Tap syringe with finger to dislodge air bubbles.
  - Aspirate to clear needle of solution.
  - Push solution up to needle hub.
  - Tip needle and syringe expelling excess solution into sink.
  - Cover and remove used needle.
  - Attach new sterile needle.
  - Read calibrations on syringe barrel at eye level to ensure correct dosage.

- Take syringe and antiseptic sponge to patient's bedside.

- Identify patient.

- Explain procedure to patient.

- Select injection site and position patient accordingly, avoiding undue exposure.

- Clean area with antiseptic sponge.

SPECIAL CONSIDERATIONS

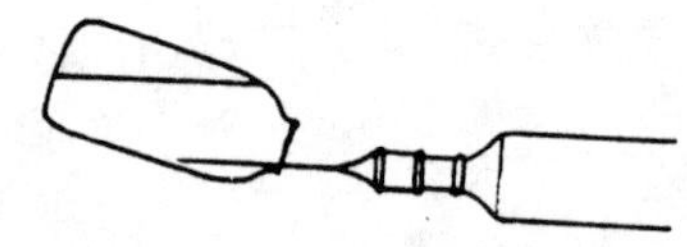

Figure 6. Withdrawing Medication from Ampule.

Do not allow solution to run down shaft of needle.

REFER TO SPECIFIC PROCEDURE: INTRAMUSCULAR, Z-TRACT, INTRADERMAL, INTRAVENOUS, SUBCUTANEOUS, OR INSULIN. After performing specific procedure continue as follows.

- Clip off needle and tip of syringe then discard.

B. *Intramuscular* (IM)

PURPOSE

To administer sterile medications intramuscularly

PROCEDURE

- See "Injections, General."
- Select injection site. See figure 7.

SPECIAL CONSIDERATIONS

Preferred site is the ventral gluteal area.

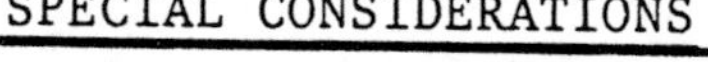

- Position patient.
  - Place on abdomen "toeing in" for gluteal area.
  - Place on side for ventral gluteal area.
- Clean area with antiseptic sponge.
- Hold tissue taut and insert needle at 90° angle as shown in figure 8.
- Aspirate. If blood appears
  - withdraw needle
  - discard medication
  - prepare new dose
- Inject medication slowly.
- Remove needle quickly while holding skin taut.
- Place antiseptic sponge over injection site exerting slight pressure.

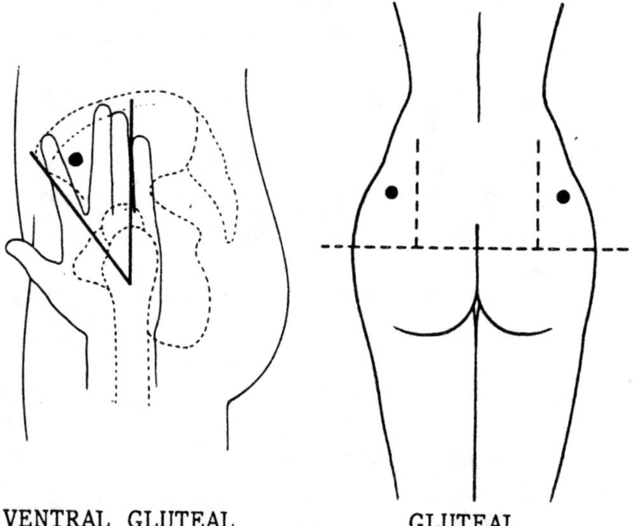

Figure 7. Intramuscular Injection Sites.

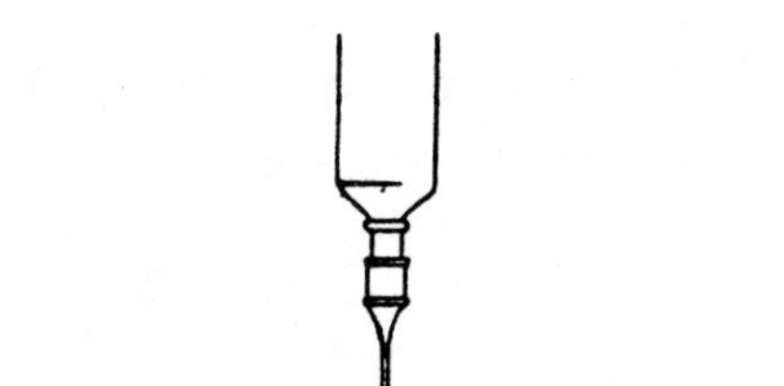

Figure 8. Intramuscular Injection Angle.

SUPPLIES AND EQUIPMENT

Antiseptic sponges (2)

Syringe, 1 to 5 ml

Needle, 21 or 22 ga, 1 1/4 ga

1. Z-Tract

PURPOSE

To prevent backflow of medication from IM injection into subcutaneous tissue

PROCEDURE

- See "Injections, General."
- Position patient.
  - Place on abdomen "toeing in" for gluteal area.
  - Place on back for vastus lateralis area.
  - Place on side for ventral gluteal area.
- Clean area with antiseptic sponge.
- Pull skin downward or to the side and insert the needle proximal to midmuscle mass downward at an oblique angle.
- Insert needle quickly with bevel up.
- Aspirate. If blood appears
  - withdraw needle
  - discard medication
  - prepare new dose
- Inject medication slowly and empty syringe completely.
- Remove needle quickly, holding skin taut.
- Release skin and wipe area with antiseptic sponge.

SPECIAL CONSIDERATIONS

C. *Intradermal* (ID)

PURPOSE

To test for sensitivity to foreign substances

PROCEDURE

- See "Injections, General."
- Select injection site.
- Clean area with antiseptic sponge.

SPECIAL CONSIDERATIONS

Usual dose for ID testing is 0.1 ml or less.

PROCEDURE

• Grasp forearm securely on both sides of injection site.
  • Place thumb on one side and forefinger on the other.
  • Hold skin taut.

• Insert needle just under skin surface at a 15° angle with bevel up. See figure 9.

• Inject solution slowly to produce a bubble or wheal.

• Remove needle.

• Read skin test.

SPECIAL CONSIDERATIONS

Figure 9. Intradermal Injection Angle.

Do not massage.

Follow local policy.

SUPPLIES AND EQUIPMENT

Antiseptic sponges (2)

Needle, 26 or 27 ga, 1 in

Syringe, TB

D. *Intravenous Piggyback* (IVPB)

PURPOSE

To administer medications through an IV line

PROCEDURE

• See "Guidelines for Medication Administration, General."

• Units with IV admixture

  • Check for correctness of medication as in guidelines above.

• Units without IV admixture

  • Prepare medications and draw into syringe.
  • Obtain secondary IV solution ensuring compatibility with medication.
  • Inject medication into secondary IV solution.
  • Label solution with
    . name of medication
    . dosage
    . date
    . time
    . your initials

SPECIAL CONSIDERATIONS

Pharmacy may prepare fluids with added medications.

Do not cover manufacturer's label.

INJECTIONS, IVPB (cont)

PROCEDURE	SPECIAL CONSIDERATIONS
• Close regulator clamp on IVPB administration set.	
• Insert piercing pin through stopper.	Maintain aseptic technique.
• Attach needle to tubing.	Local policy dictates size of needle.
• Clear air from tubing and needle.	
• Label tubing with • date • time • your initials	Tubing and needle must be changed every 24 hours.
• Take equipment to bedside.	
• Identify patient as in guidelines above.	
• Have secondary IV on standard.	
• Clean upper Y-junction on primary IV set with alcohol swab.	
• Insert secondary needle into Y.	
• Secure needle with tape.	
• Open clamp on secondary set and adjust rate.	Primary and secondary IVs run simultaneously. IVPBs may not run unless primary bottle is lower. It is not necessary to adjust flow rate of primary bottle. It will begin again when IVPB is empty.
• Record amount of fluid infused on I&O worksheet.	
• Record medication on MAR.	

SUPPLIES AND EQUIPMENT

Adhesive tape	IV administration set	Label
Alcohol swabs	IV solution (50 to 150 ml)	Needle, 23 to 19 ga

E. *Subcutaneous* (SC)

PURPOSE

To administer medications subcutaneously

PROCEDURE

- See "Injections, General."
- Select injection site. See figure 10.
- Clean area with antiseptic sponge.
- Pinch skin between thumb and forefinger.
- Insert needle at 45° angle with bevel up as shown in figure 11.
- Aspirate. If blood appears
  - withdraw needle
  - discard medication
  - prepare new dose
- Inject medication slowly.
- Withdraw needle quickly.
- Place antiseptic sponge over site and apply gentle pressure.

SPECIAL CONSIDERATIONS

Another acceptable site is the anterior lateral aspect of the thigh.

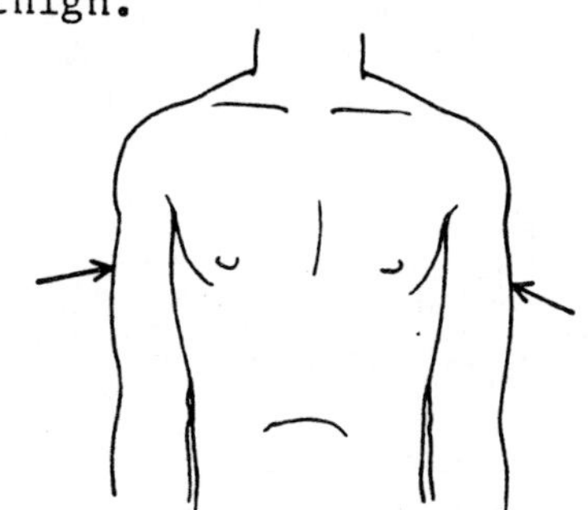

Figure 10. Subcutaneous Injection Site.

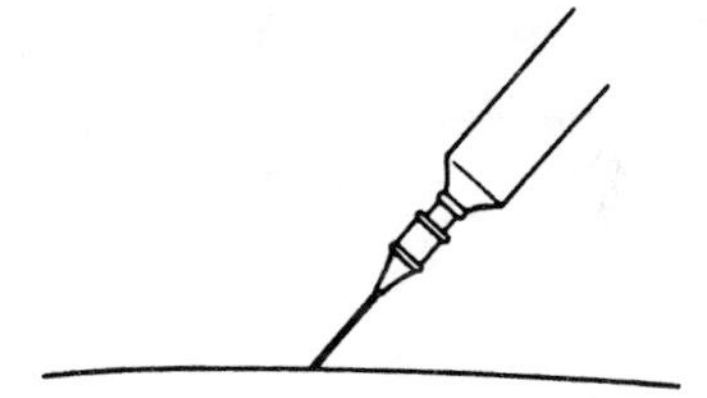

Figure 11. Subcutaneous Injection Angle.

SUPPLIES AND EQUIPMENT

Antiseptic sponges (2) Needle, 23 ga, 3/4 in Syringe, 2 1/2 ml

1. *Insulin*

PURPOSE

To lower blood sugar

PROCEDURE

- See "Injections, General."
- Roll insulin vial between palms to thoroughly mix and warm.

SPECIAL CONSIDERATIONS

INJECTIONS, SC, Insulin (cont)

PROCEDURE

• Have another person (nurse) check dose you prepare.

• Select injection site. See figure 12.
  • Rotate injection sites systematically as directed by local policy.

• Clean area with antiseptic sponge.

• Pinch skin between thumb and forefinger.

• Insert needle at 45° angle with bevel up (fig. 11).

• Aspirate. If blood appears
  • withdraw needle
  • discard medication
  • prepare new dose

• Inject medication slowly.

• Withdraw needle quickly.

• Place antiseptic sponge over site and apply gentle pressure.

SPECIAL CONSIDERATIONS

Do not give to an NPO patient without consulting physician for specific instructions.

Absorption from the arm is more rapid than from the thigh.

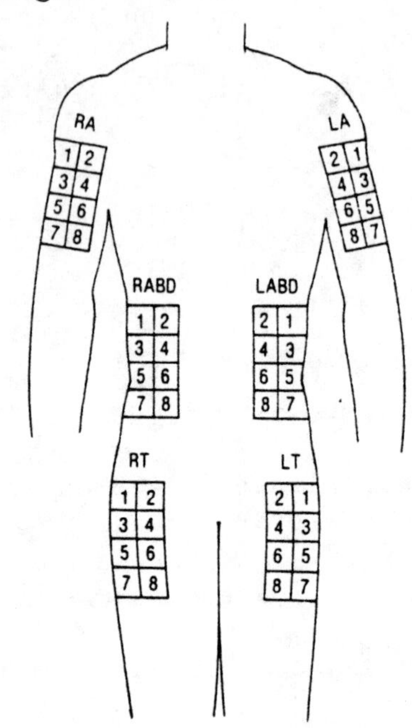

Figure 12. Insulin Injection Sites.

SUPPLIES AND EQUIPMENT

Needle, 23 ga, 3/4 in

Syringe, insulin

VII. *ORAL MEDICATIONS*

PURPOSE

To prepare and administer medications orally

PROCEDURE

• See "Guidelines for Medication Administration, General."

SPECIAL CONSIDERATIONS

PROCEDURE	SPECIAL CONSIDERATIONS

A. Tablets, Pills, or Capsules

- Instruct patient how to take medication.

  For example, if medication is given sublingually, let pill dissolve under tongue.

- Check apical pulse rate for 1 full minute before giving cardiotonics.
  - Do not give if rate is below 60 per minute.
  - Notify nurse or physician.
  - Record on MAR.

B. Powders

- Remove powdered medications from container with a clean, dry, tongue depressor.

C. Liquids

- Shake medication if it is a precipitate.
- Remove bottle cap and place on counter inside up.
- Hold bottle with label covered by your palm to prevent soiling label.
- Measure liquids at eye level using calibrated medication cup.
- Wipe rim of bottle before recapping.
- If medication is ordered in drops, count them aloud.
- Dilute irons, acids, and iodides in 120 ml water and have patient drink through straw.
  - Irons and iodides stain teeth.
  - Acids and iodides can irritate mouth.
- Give cough medications after all others are taken.

  Do not dilute or give water following liquid cough medications.

VIII. *SUPPOSITORIES*

A. *Rectal*

PURPOSE

To administer medication rectally

PROCEDURE	SPECIAL CONSIDERATIONS
• See "Guidelines for Medication Administration, General."	
• Screen patient.	
• Place patient in left Sim's position.	
• Remove protective wrapper from medication.	
• Don finger cot or disposable glove.	
• Separate buttocks.	
• Insert suppository gently through anal opening about 2 inches, using index finger.	
• Have patient try to retain suppository for 20 minutes if given to cause bowel movement.	Others can be retained indefinitely.
• Hold buttocks together for a minute or two to ensure absorption.	
• Remove glove or finger cot and discard.	
• Wash your hands.	
• Assist patient to a comfortable position as needed.	

SUPPLIES AND EQUIPMENT

Finger cot or glove

B. *Urethral*

PURPOSE

To administer medication through the urethra

PROCEDURE

- See "Guidelines for Medication Administration, General."
- Screen patient.

Females

- Place patient on back, legs drawn up and apart, with perineum exposed.
- Remove suppository from wrapper.
- Don disposable glove.
- Separate labia with thumb and forefinger and insert suppository. See figure 13.
- Remove glove and discard.
- Wash your hands.

Males

- Place patient on back with perineum exposed.
- Remove suppository from wrapper.
- Don disposable glove.
- Grasp penis with thumb and forefinger of one hand to expose meatus.
- Insert suppository.
- Remove glove and discard.
- Wash your hands.

SPECIAL CONSIDERATIONS

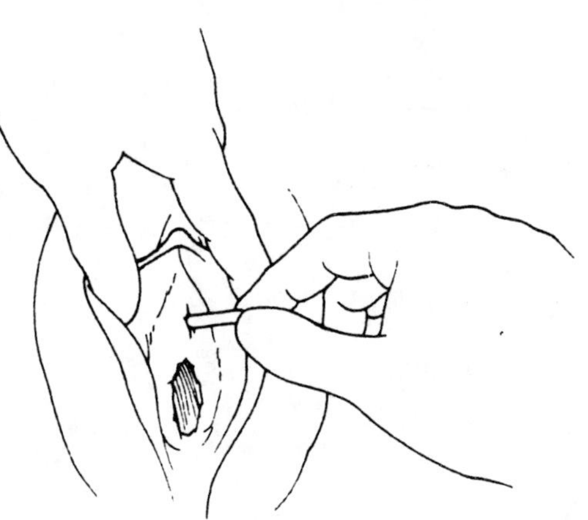

Figure 13. Inserting a Urethral Suppository.

Replace foreskin in uncircumcised males to prevent constriction.

SUPPLIES AND EQUIPMENT

Glove, disposable

C. *Vaginal*

PURPOSE

To administer medication vaginally

PROCEDURE

SPECIAL CONSIDERATIONS

- See "Guidelines for Medication Administration, General."
- Screen patient.
- Position patient in dorsal lithotomy position and expose perineum.
- Remove suppository from wrapper.
- Don disposable glove.
- Separate labia with thumb and forefinger.
- Insert suppository about 2 inches upward and backward into vagina.
- Remove glove and discard.
- Assist patient to comfortable position as needed.
- Wash your hands.

SUPPLIES AND EQUIPMENT

Finger cot or glove

MEDICAL / NURSING SCIENCE

DIAGNOSTIC TESTS AND PROCEDURES

CONTENTS

Page

I. TECHNIQUE OF VENIPUNCTURE 1

II. TECHNIQUE OF VENIPUNCTURE WITH VACUTAINER 4

III. COLLECTION OF SPECIMENS 6
- A. Blood Culture 6
- B. Blood/Bromsulphalein Test 7
- C. Blood and Urine/Glucose Tolerance Test 8
- D. Urine 10
- E. Midstream or Clean-Catch Urine 11
- F. Urine/24-Hour Collection 12
- G. Urine/Reagent Test for Sugar 13
- H. Urine/Reagent Test for Acetone/Acetest 15
- I. Urine/Urobilinogen 16
- J. Urine/Addis Sediment Count 17
- K. Urine/Fishberg Concentration Test 18
- L. Urine/24-Hour Urine for Vanlmandelu Acid (VMA) 19
- M. Urine/Phenolsulfonphthalein Excretion Test(PSP Test) 20
- N. Sputum 21
- O. Gastric Analysis 22
- P. Feces 24
- Q. Guiac Test 25
- R. Rectal Swab 26
- S. Discharges from Wounds or Cavities/Smear 27
- T. Discharges from Wounds or Cavities/Culture 28

IV. PREPARATION FOR RADIOLOGICAL STUDIES 29
- A. Angiocardiography 29
- B. Arteriography (Cerebral) 30
- C. Bronchogram 31
- D. Cholecystography (Gallbladder Series) 32
- E. Gastrointestinal Series 33
- F. Barium Enema 34
- G. Intravenous Pyelogram 35
- H. Myelogram 36
- I. Pneumoencephalogram 37

V. BRONCHOSCOPY 38

VI. T-3, T-4 TEST 39

VII. COLD PRESSOR TEST 40

VIII. ABDOMINAL PARACENTESIS 41

IX. LUMBAR PUNCTURE 43

X. THORACENTESIS 45

MEDICAL / NURSING SCIENCE

DIAGNOSTIC TESTS AND PROCEDURES

I. TECHNIQUE OF VENIPUNCTURE

PURPOSE

To obtain a specimen of blood for laboratory examination.

EQUIPMENT

Tray with:
- Tourniquet
- Sterile syringe - size as needed
- Sterile needles - 20 - 21 gauge, 1 1/4" length
- Alcohol sponges
- Tube for blood specimen
- Sterile 2 x 2 gauze sponge

PROCEDURE

1. Wash hands.
2. Assemble equipment.
3. Explain procedure to the patient.
4. Apply tourniquet firmly about upper arm.
5. Select a vein in arm which can be seen and easily palpated.
6. Cleanse skin with alcohol sponge.
7. Hold patient's arm extended with little or no flexion at elbow.
8. Hold syringe firmly. Enter vein with bevel of needle uppermost.
9. Withdraw blood sample.
10. Release tourniquet.
11. Place dry sponge over puncture site. Withdraw needle. Apply pressure.
12. Inject blood from syringe into proper blood tube for diagnostic procedure.

POINTS TO EMPHASIZE

1. If needle fails to enter vein, it may be withdrawn slightly. Keep point well under the skin, and again direct toward vein.
2. Report if you are unsuccessful in obtaining a specimen or entering a vein after 2 attempts. Do Not Continue.
3. Blood cannot flow into arm and fill veins if the tourniquet has been applied too tightly.
4. A blood pressure cuff with manometer may be used in place of a tourniquet.
5. A sterilized syringe and needle are used for each patient.

POINTS TO EMPHASIZE (Continued)

6. Identify patient before taking specimen by checking bed tag, identification band, and asking patient his name.
7. To prevent hemolysis:
   a. Use dry syringe and tube.
   b. On oxalated blood, agitate gently immediately after introducing into bottle.
8. Label each specimen container with patient's identifying data.
9. Allow alcohol to dry on patient's skin prior to venipuncture to reduce pain.

CARE OF EQUIPMENT

1. Break off tips of needle and syringe.
2. Dispose of needle and syringe according to local instructions.

TECHNIQUE OF VENIPUNCTURE (Continued)

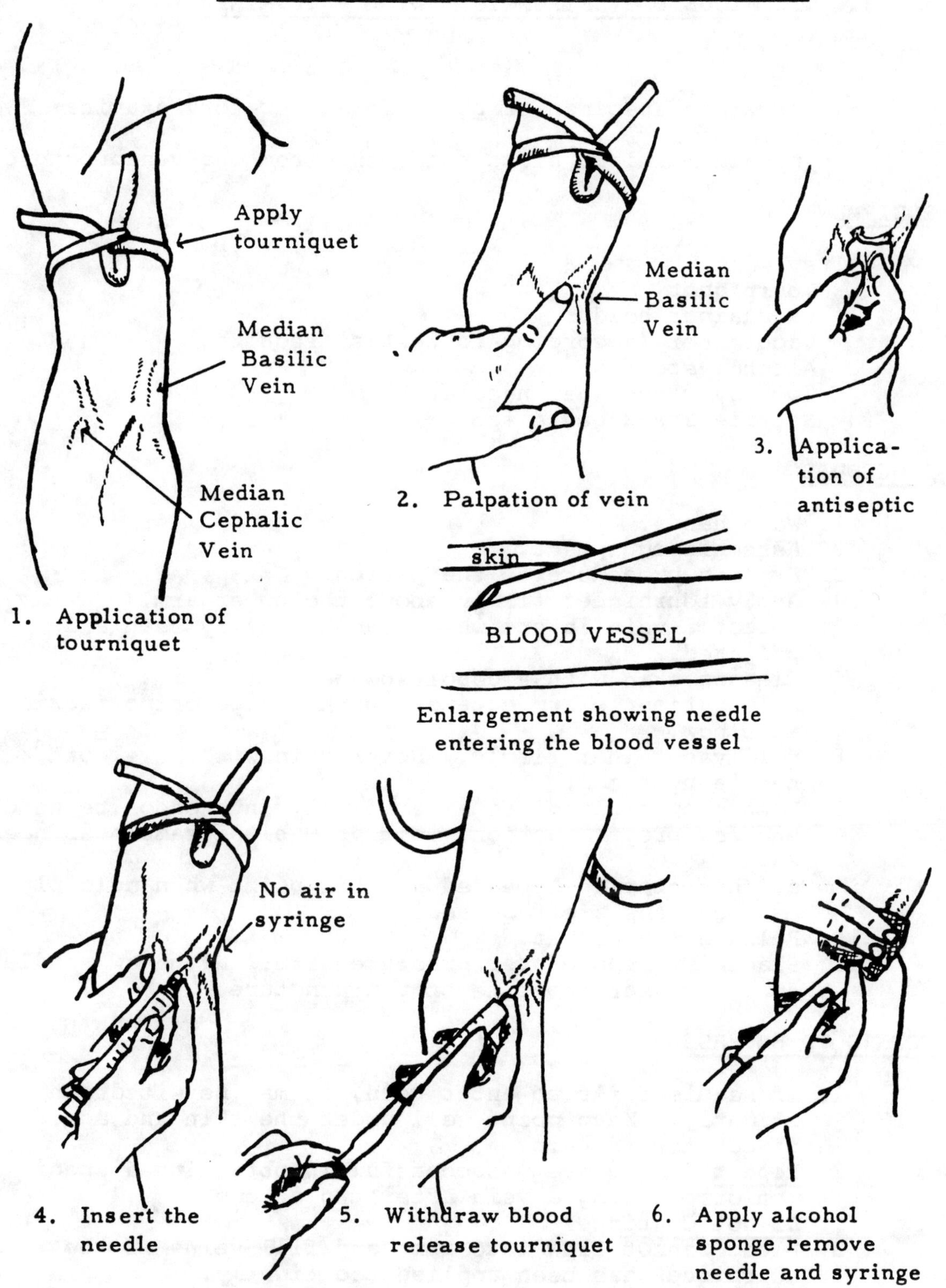

Enlargement showing needle entering the blood vessel

II. TECHNIQUE OF VENIPUNCTURE WITH VACUTAINER

PURPOSE

To obtain a specimen of blood for laboratory examination.
To obtain multiple blood specimens from one venipuncture.

EQUIPMENT

Tray with
- Tourniquet
- Vacutainer holder
- Vacutainer (according to test(s) required)
- Alcohol sponges
- Two way vacutainer needles
- Sterile 2 x 2 gauze sponge

PROCEDURE

1. Wash hands.
2. Assemble equipment.
3. Explain procedure to the patient.
4. Apply tourniquet firmly about the upper arm.
5. Select a vein in arm which can be easily seen and palpated.
6. Cleanse skin with alcohol sponge.
7. Hold patient's arm extended with little or no flexion at elbow.
8. Hold vacutainer firmly. Enter vein with bevel of needle uppermost.
9. Push proper blood container firmly into opposite needle end for proper suction. Withdraw blood sample as needed.
   a. This step is repeated at this point when multiple specimens are required.
10. Release tourniquet.
11. Place dry sponge over puncture site. Withdraw needle. Apply pressure to site of venipuncture.

POINTS TO EMPHASIZE

1. If needle fails to enter vein, it may be withdrawn slightly. Keep point well under the skin and again direct toward vein.
2. Report if you are unsuccessful in obtaining a specimen or entering a vein after two attempts. Do Not Continue.
3. Blood cannot flow into arms and fill veins if the tourniquet has been applied too tightly.
4. A blood pressure cuff with manometer may be used in place of a tourniquet.
5. A sterile vacutainer needle is used for each patient.
6. Allow alcohol to dry on skin prior to venipuncture to reduce pain.

VACUTAINER

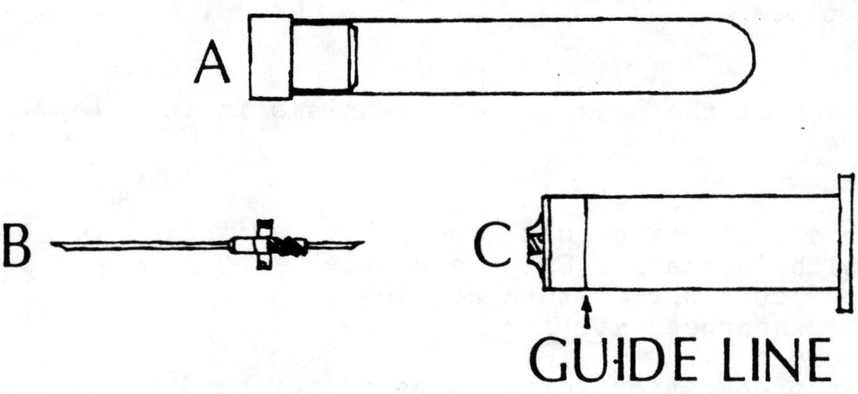

PARTS

A. EVACUATED GLASS TUBE WITH RUBBER STOPPER
B. DOUBLE POINTED NEEDLE
C. PLASTIC HOLDER

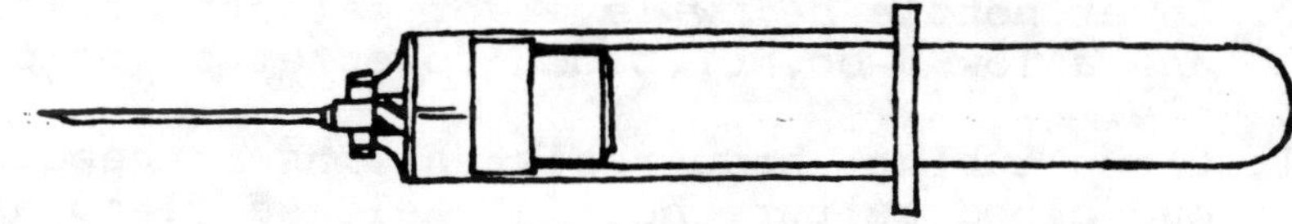

TO ASSEMBLE VACUTAINER

1. THREAD NEEDLE INTO HOLDER
2. PLACE TUBE IN HOLDER WITH NEEDLE TOUCHING STOPPER
3. PUSH TUBE FORWARD UNTIL TOP OF STOPPER MEETS GUIDE LINE

III. COLLECTION OF SPECIMENS

A. BLOOD CULTURE

(Using Vacutainer Bottle)

PURPOSE

To detect the presence of organisms in the blood.

EQUIPMENT

Blood collecting unit especially designated to go with Vacutainer Culture Bottle
Two Vacutainer Culture Bottles
2 x 2 sponges, sterile
Hemostat
Skin preparation solution as prescribed
Bacteriology form for aerobic and anaerobic specimens

PROCEDURE

1. Wash hands.
2. Explain procedure to patient.
3. Prep site with solution prescribed by local policy.
4. Assemble vacutainer as directed.
5. Be sure tubing from vacutainer to needle is clamped.
6. Execute venipuncture.
7. Remove or have assistant remove cap from blood culture bottle (outer cap only).
8. Remove cap from short needle.
9. Insert needle into blood culture bottle for anaerobic specimen.
10. Lower bottle below level of patient, release clamp and allow 5 cc. of blood to enter blood culture bottle.
11. Clamp tubing, have assistant insert needle into second blood culture bottle. Release clamp and allow 5 cc. of blood to drain into second bottle.
12. Release tourniquet.
13. Place dry sponge over puncture site.
14. Remove needle from arm, let air into bottle for aerobic specimen.
15. Submit specimens with properly labelled chits to bacteriology laboratory immediately.

POINTS TO EMPHASIZE

1. Contamination of the blood from skin, apparatus, container of air will render this test ineffective.
2. Tourniquet must be tight enough to obstruct venous flow but not cause discoloration of extremity.
3. If patient is on antibiotic therapy, drugs must be listed on bacteriology chit.

COLLECTION OF SPECIMENS
B. BLOOD
BROMSULPHALEIN TEST

PURPOSE

To determine liver function.

EQUIPMENT

BSP dye
Two sterile syringes; 10 cc. and 18 gauge needles
Tourniquet
One sterile test tube without anticoagulant
SF 546, Blood Chemistry

PROCEDURE

1. Explain procedure. Tell patient what he is to do.
2. Instruct patient to:
   a. Take nothing by mouth after 2400 hours.
   b. Delay breakfast until after the test.
3. Weigh patient at 0600 and divide weight by 2.2 to determine the patient's weight in kilograms. The amount of dye to be injected by the medical officer is calculated on the basis of the patient's weight in kilograms. (5 mg. of dye per kilogram of body weight.)
4. Have dye ready for medical officer. Record time given on SF 546 and record procedure on Nursing Notes (SF 510).
5. Draw blood sample from opposite arm of injection 45 minutes following injection of dye.

POINTS TO EMPHASIZE

1. Use separate syringe and needle for injection and taking blood samples.
2. Amount of dye injected is determined by patient's weight in kilograms. The dosage is verified by the medical officer injecting the dye.

CARE OF EQUIPMENT

1. Break tips of needles and syringes.
2. Discard disposable needle and tubing according to local instructions.

COLLECTION OF SPECIMENS
C. BLOOD AND URINE
GLUCOSE TOLERANCE TEST

PURPOSE

To assist in detection and diagnosis of diabetes mellitus or other liver disturbances.

EQUIPMENT

NPO sign
Tray containing:
- Five sterile 10 cc. syringes
- Five sterile 20 or 21 gauge, 1 1/4" length needles
- Tourniquet
- Alcohol sponges
- Glucose preparation as ordered
- Five (oxalate) gray top tubes with labels
- Five urine specimen bottles with labels
- Rubber bands
- Standard Form 550, Urinalysis
- Standard Form 546, Blood Chemistry

PROCEDURE

1. Explain procedure. Tell patient what he is to do.
2. Patient is to have nothing by mouth after 1900 the day preceding test.
3. A fasting blood specimen is drawn and a urine sample is collected for a control specimen upon arising. Label Specimen #1.
4. Patient drinks a glucose and water diet containing 1 gram of glucose per kilogram of body weight.
5. Collect urine specimens and 5 cc. blood specimens after ingestion of glucose, as follows:
   a. Specimen #2 - one half hour interval.
   b. Specimen #3 - one hour interval.
   c. Specimen #4 - two hours interval.
   d. Specimen #5 - three hours interval.
6. Hold all urine and blood specimens until test is completed. Send to laboratory marked with appropriate forms.
7. Record procedure on the Nursing Notes (SF 510).

POINTS TO EMPHASIZE

1. Label specimen bottle and tubes in advance with patient's identification and specimen number. Record time specimen is obtained on appropriate label.

COLLECTION OF SPECIMENS (Continued)
BLOOD AND URINE
GLUCOSE TOLERANCE TEST (Continued)

POINTS TO EMPHASIZE (Continued)

2. Patient may drink water after the one-hour specimen has been collected.
3. Ambulatory patients may go to the laboratory for entire test.

CARE OF EQUIPMENT

1. Break off tips of needle and syringes.
2. Discard needles and syringes according to local instruction.

COLLECTION OF SPECIMENS
D. URINE

Single Clean Specimen

PURPOSE

To obtain a specimen of urine for routine and miscroscopic examination

EQUIPMENT

Clean urinal or bedpan
Urine specimen bottle with cap
Rubber band
Standard Form 550, Urinalysis

PROCEDURE

1. Tell patient what he is to do.
2. Have patient void into clean bedpan or urinal.
3. Pour sample (120-155 cc.) into specimen bottle. Cap.
4. Wrap request around bottle. Hold in place with rubber band.
5. Send specimen to laboratory with SF 550.

Single Sterile Specimen

PURPOSE

To obtain specimen of urine for bacteriological and other examinations.

EQUIPMENT

Catheterization tray
Sterile gloves
Sterile specimen bottle
Rubber band
Standard Form 550, Urinalysis

PROCEDURE

1. Catheterize patient.
2. Collect urine directly from catheter into sterile bottle. Cover with sterile gauze or sterile cap.
3. Wrap request around bottle. Hold in place with rubber band.
4. Send specimen to laboratory.

COLLECTION OF SPECIMENS (Continued)

E. MIDSTREAM OR CLEAN-CATCH URINE

PURPOSE

To obtain a clean specimen of urine for laboratory analysis.

EQUIPMENT

Sterile urine bottle and cap
4 x 4 gauze sponges, sterile
Disinfectant as ordered by local command

PROCEDURE (MALE)

1. Instruct patient to:
   a. Wash penis using 4 x 4s and disinfectant ordered. (Cleanse well around foreskin and meatus.)
   b. Void small amount of urine into toilet and then void directly into sterile bottle.
2. Place sterile cap on bottle.
3. Wrap request around bottle and secure with rubber band.
4. Send specimen to laboratory.

PROCEDURE (FEMALE)

1. Instruct patient to:
   a. Wash genitalia using 4 x 4s and disinfectant.
   b. During voiding hold labia apart.
   c. Void small amount of urine into toilet and then void directly into sterile bottle.
2. Place sterile cap on bottle.
3. Wrap request around bottle and secure with rubber band.
4. Send specimen to laboratory.

POINTS TO EMPHASIZE

1. Discard 4 x 4s into waste receptacle.
2. Thorough cleansing of external genitalia is essential.
3. Patient must void first portion of specimen into toilet.
4. Urine specimens should be sent to the laboratory as soon as possible because urinary sediments are greatly altered by time.

COLLECTION OF SPECIMENS (Continued)
F. URINE

24 - HOUR COLLECTION -- QUANTITATIVE SPECIMEN

PURPOSE

To obtain all urine produced by the kidney over a 24-hour period of time for the purpose of studying kidney function.

EQUIPMENT

Urinal or bedpan
Large container and cover
Shipping tag
Standard Form 550, Urinalysis

PROCEDURE

1. Label bottle - include patient's name, rate, date, ward, type of specimen.
2. Explain procedure. Tell patient what he is to do.
3. Ask patient to void at 0600. Discard specimen.
4. Collect all urine voided for 24 hours in bottle.
5. Ask patient to void at 0600 following morning. Add to bottle. If unable to void, obtain order for catheterization.
6. Send entire specimen to laboratory with SF 550.

COLLECTION OF SPECIMENS (Continued)

G. URINE

REAGENT TEST FOR SUGAR

PURPOSE

To determine the amount of sugar, if any, contained in the patient's urine.

CLINITEST

EQUIPMENT

Clinitest Reagent Tablet
Bedpan or urinal
Test tube and holder
Medicine dropper
Clinitest Color Chart

PROCEDURE

1. Ask patient to void.
2. Place 5 drops of urine in clean test tube with medicine dropper. Rinse dropper.
3. Add 10 drops of water to test tube.
4. Place test tube in holder as chemical reaction causes heat.
5. Drop in one Clinitest Tablet. Watch solution boil.
6. Wait 15 seconds after boiling stops. Gently shake tube.
7. Hold test tube next to color chart and compare:
   a. All shades of blue. . . . . Negative for sugar
   b. Green. . . . . .1 plus for sugar
   c. Olive tan. . . . . .2 plus for sugar
   d. Orange. . . . . 3 plus for sugar
   e. Brown. . . . . .4 plus for sugar
8. Record result of test on Nursing Notes (SF 510) and/or Diabetic Flow sheet.

POINTS TO EMPHASIZE

1. Clinitest Color Chart must be used with Clinitest Tablets.
2. Do not touch Clinitest Tablets with fingers, for moisture initiates a chemical reaction producing heat.
3. Keep cap of bottle of Clinitest Tablets tightly closed to prevent decompensation.
4. A double voided may be ordered. This refers to a specimen obtained 30 minutes after the patient emties his bladder.

CLINISTIX

EQUIPMENT

Bedpan or urinal
Clinistix
Clinistix Color Chart

PROCEDURE

1. Ask patient to void.
2. Dip test end of strip into urine and remove.
3. Wait exactly one minute.
4. Compare both sides of strip with Clinistix Color Chart:
   a. No blue color - negative for sugar
   b. Light blue - 1 plus for sugar
   c. Medium blue - 2 plus for sugar
   d. Dark blue - 3 plus for sugar
5. Record results of test on Nursing Notes (SF 510) and/or Diabetic Flow Sheet.

TES-TAPE

EQUIPMENT

Bedpan or urinal
Tes-Tape
Tes-Tape Color chart

PROCEDURE

1. Ask patient to void.
2. Cut one and one-half inch (1 1/2) strip from Tes-Tape roll.
3. Dip Tes-Tape strip in urine and remove.
4. Wait exactly one minute.
5. Compare with Tes-Tape Color Chart on side of container.
   a. Yellow - negative
   b. Light green - 1 plus for sugar
   c. Olive green - 2 plus for sugar
   d. Medium green - 3 plus for sugar
   e. Dark green - 4 plus for sugar
6. Record result of test on Nursing Notes (SF 510) and/or Diabetic Flow Sheet.

COLLECTION OF SPECIMENS (Continued)

H. URINE

REAGENT TEST FOR ACETONE

ACETEST

PURPOSE

To determine the amount, if any, of acetone contained in the urine.

EQUIPMENT

Bedpan or urinal
Medicine dropper
Acetest Reagent Powder
Filter paper or paper towel
Color Chart

PROCEDURE

1. Ask patient to void. Discard specimen.
2. Ask patient to void one-half hour later. Save specimen for test.
3. Place small amount of Acetest Powder on filter paper or on paper towel. (One Acetest Tablet may be used.
4. Place one or two drops of urine on Acetest Powder/ Tablet. Wait 30 seconds.
5. No change in color indicates a negative result; lavender or deep purple indicates a positive test.
6. Record result of test on Nursing Notes (SF 510) and/or Diabetic Flow Sheet.

CARE OF EQUIPMENT

Discard specimen; clean and return equipment to proper place.

COLLECTION OF SPECIMENS (Continued)
I. URINE
UROBILINOGEN

PURPOSE

To determine the amount of bile (if any) in the urine.

EQUIPMENT

Urine specimen bottle and cap
Standard Form, 550 Urinalysis

PROCEDURE

1. Tell patient what he is to do.
2. Have patient void at specified time. Discard specimen.
3. Instruct patient to drink a glass of water.
4. Collect specimen two hours later.
5. Send to laboratory immediately with SF 550.

COLLECTION OF SPECIMENS (Continued)
J. URINE
ADDIS SEDIMENT COUNT

PURPOSE

To calculate the total urinary sediment in a twelve hour specimen.

EQUIPMENT

Wide-mouth bottle from laboratory
Standard Form 550, Urinalysis

PROCEDURE

1. Explain procedure. Tell patient what he is to do.
2. Patient may have usual breakfast.
3. Withhold fluids in any form for next 24 hours. May have diet except fluids and fruit.
4. Ask patient to void at 2000 hours. Discard specimen. Record time bladder was emptied on laboratory chit. Ask patient not to void for next 12 hours. If he must void during this period, urine must be saved.
5. Ask patient to void into container at 0800 the next morning and record on the label the exact time of voiding.
6. Cover container and send specimen to laboratory with request, specifying name of test and exact time of collection.

POINTS TO EMPHASIZE

1. The time interval is important.
2. A 12 hour night specimen is the requirement.

COLLECTION OF SPECIMENS (Continued)
K. URINE
FISHBERG CONCENTRATION TEST

PURPOSE

To determine the specific gravity of urine.

EQUIPMENT

Three urine specimen bottles with labels
Standard Form 548, Renal Function

PROCEDURE

1. Explain procedure. Tell patient what he is to do.
2. On day before test:
   a. Patient may have usual lunch. Dry evening meal.
   b. Withhold all fluids for 17 hours prior to collecting the first specimen.
   c. Nothing by mouth after 2400 hours.
   d. Have patient void before retiring. This specimen and any urine voided during night is discarded.
3. Collect specimen #1 at 0500, while patient is in bed. Record time of voiding on specimen label.
4. Collect specimen #2 at 0600 while patient is in bed. Record time of voiding on label.
5. Ask patient to get out of bed and move about ward for one hour.
6. Collect specimen #3 at 0700. Record time of voiding on label.
7. Send specimens to laboratory with SF 548.
8. Serve patient breakfast.

POINTS TO EMPHASIZE

Patient remains in bed until after Specimen #2 is collected.

L. URINE

24 HOUR URINE FOR VANLMANDELU ACID (Continued)
(VMA)

PURPOSE

A screening test to assist the doctor in the diagnosis of Pheochromorytoma. The major symptom of this disease is hypertension.

EQUIPMENT

24 hour urine container with acidic preservative.
(Obtain container from laboratory)
Standard Form 548, CHEM III (Urine)

PROCEDURE

1. Explain procedure. Tell patient when and what he is to do.
2. All medications are withheld for 48 hours before beginning the urine collection and during the collection period.
3. VMA diet 48 hours prior to and during collection of urine. This is a Regular Diet which excludes the following: NO coffee, tea, chocolate, bananas, avocados, nuts, vanilla, or citrus fruits.
4. Have patient void on morning of test before breakfast. Discard this specimen. Record time of voiding.
5. All urine during the next 24 hours is collected in special container with preservative.
6. During the collection period the bottle containing the urine must be protected from sunlight.
7. At the end of the collection period the entire 24 hour specimen is sent to the laboratory properly labeled.

POINTS TO EMPHASIZE

1. Invalid test results will be obtained if dietary and medication restrictions are not followed.
2. Care should be taken to avoid contact of preservative solution with skin since it is an acid.

COLLECTION OF SPECIMENS (Continued)
M. URINE
PHENOLSULFONPHTHALEIN EXCRETION TEST
PSP TEST

PURPOSE

To determine kidney function.

EQUIPMENT

Sterile tuberculin syringe
Sterile 20 or 21 gauge, 1 1/4" length needle
Alcohol sponges
Ampule of Phenolsulfonphthalein Dye (6 mg.)
Tourniquet
Four labeled urine specimen bottles and caps
Standard Form 548, Renal Function

PROCEDURE

1. Tell patient what he is to do.
2. Give patient two glasses of water one hour before test. Instruct him not to void.
3. Draw up one cc. of PSP dye into tuberculin syringe.
4. Note exact time the medical officer injects dye intravenously.
5. Exactly 15 minutes after dye has been injected, have patient void completely emptying his bladder. Save entire amount. Label 15 minute specimen.
6. Have patient void in 30, 60 and 120 minutes after dye injection. Save all urine voided each time. Label 30 minute, 60 minute, 120 minute specimens with exact time of voiding. Patient may have one glass of water after the 60 minute specimen is collected, if necessary.
7. Send specimens and request to laboratory.

COLLECTION OF SPECIMENS (Continued)

N. SPUTUM

PURPOSE

To collect a specimen of sputum for laboratory analysis.
To determine causative organisms in respiratory diseases.

EQUIPMENT

Sputum jar with cover
Rubber band
Standard Form 554, Bacteriology

PROCEDURE

Single Specimen

1. Administer oral hygiene or instruct patient to do so.
2. Instruct patient to cough deeply and to expectorate directly into jar.
3. Label specimen jar with patient's name and ward.
4. Attach request to covered jar with rubber band.
5. Send specimen to laboratory.

24 Hour Specimen

1. Instruct patient as to what he is to do:
   a. Expectorate all sputum directly into jar each time he coughs deeply.
   b. Cover jar each time he expectorates.
2. Start and stop collection of sputum at a definite time - 0600 - 0600 hours.
3. Send properly labeled specimen to laboratory with request chit upon completion of test.

POINTS TO EMPHASIZE

1. Instruct patient:
   a. Not to expectorate saliva into jar.
   b. To keep jar covered.
2. Indicate on SF 554 examination desired and submit request in duplicate if smear and culture is requested.
3. All 24-hour collections should begin and end at a definite time and the bottle or cover should be so marked.

COLLECTION OF SPECIMENS (Continued)

O. GASTRIC ANALYSIS

SINGLE FASTING SPECIMEN

PURPOSE

To remove gastric secretions for diagnostic studies.

EQUIPMENT

Levin tube, rubber/plastic
Basin cracked ice (omit for plastic tube)
Water soluble lubricant
Protective sheet or pad
Clean test tubes or glass specimen jars
20 or 30 cc. syringe
Curved basin
Rubber band
Standard Form 547, Gastric Analysis
Nothing by Mouth (NPO) sign

PROCEDURE

1. Explain procedure. Tell patient what he is to do.
2. Nothing by mouth after 2400 hours.
3. Place patient in sitting position to facilitate passing of tube.
4. Lubricate tip of tube with small amount of water or water soluble lubricant. Pass tube gently into patient's nostril and into nasopharynx.
5. Allow patient small piece of ice to suck on if he wishes. Tell patient to swallow while tube is being passed into stomach.
6. Observe patient's breathing and voice to tell whether tube is passing into the correct canal. If breathing or speaking becomes difficult, withdraw tube immediately.
7. When tube is in the stomach, withdraw specimen with syringe. Place specimen in tube or jar and label "Fasting".
8. The medical officer may inject alcohol or histamine through the tube into the stomach after the fasting specimen is withdrawn.
9. Continue to collect specimens every 15 minutes for one and one-half hours after the initial fasting specimen.
10. Remove Levin tube. Make patient comfortable.
11. Label each test tube or specimen jar with name of patient and time collected. Send specimen to laboratory with request.
12. Patient may have his breakfast upon completion of test.

COLLECTION OF SPECIMENS (Continued)
GASTRIC ANALYSIS

SINGLE FASTING SPECIMEN (Continued)

POINTS TO EMPHASIZE

Do not use mineral oil to lubercate tip of Levin tube.

CARE OF EQUIPMENT

1. Wash tube and syringe and return to CSR.
2. If plastic Levin tube is used, discard it.

COLLECTION OF SPECIMENS (Continued)

P. FECES

PURPOSE

To obtain a sample of feces for diagnostic study.

EQUIPMENT

Clean bedpan
Screw capped specimen jar
Two tongue blades
Rubber band
Standard Form 552, Feces

PROCEDURE WHEN TESTING FOR OVA AND PARASITES

1. Collect specimen in clean bedpan.
2. Take bedpan to utility room.
3. Remove approximately one ounce of feces from pan with tongue blades. Place in jar. Cover.
4. Attach request to jar and secure with rubber band.
5. Send specimen to laboratory immediately with SF 552.

PROCEDURE WHEN EXAMINING FOR OCCULT BLOOD

1. Patient is placed on a meat-free diet two days before specimen is collected.
2. Collection procedure is same as above.

PROCEDURE OCCULT BLOOD - ALTERNATE

1. Obtain stock MF (merthiolate formaldehyde) tube from laboratory.
2. Place fecal sample (about size of a pea) in tube.
3. Insert stopper in tube. Send to laboratory with SF 552 in duplicate.

PROCEDURE WHEN EXAMINING FOR AMOEBA

1. Remove feces from pan with tongue blades. Place in jar and cover.
2. Send warm specimen with request to laboratory immediately. If unable to send specimen immediately, place jar in basin of warm water.
3. Record on SF 552 the time the specimen was passed.

POINTS TO EMPHASIZE

Specimen to be examined for amoeba must be kept warm and sent to laboratory immediately.

COLLECTION OF SPECIMENS (Continued)

Q. GUIAC TEST

PURPOSE

To test stool specimen for blood.

EQUIPMENT

Three bottles with droppers containing:
- (1) Acetic acid solution 10%
- (2) Saturated solution of guiac
- (3) Hydrogen peroxide 3%

Clean glass slide
Application stick
Watch with second hand

PROCEDURE

1. Place two drops of each solution on glass slide. Do not mix solutions.
2. With applicator stick place small amount of feces on glass slide and mix with solutions.
3. Read results within 30 seconds.
4. A blue-green color is reported as positive; otherwise, the report is negative.
5. Record results on Nursing Notes (SF 510) and/or flow sheet.

POINTS TO EMPHASIZE

1. Solutions must be fresh.
2. Do not mix solutions until after feces has been added.

CARE OF EQUIPMENT

1. Discard applicator and slide.
2. Replace equipment.

R. RECTAL SWAB

PURPOSE

To obtain specimen for detection of worms.

EQUIPMENT

Rectal swab in broth obtained from laboratory

PROCEDURE

1. Explain procedure to patient if old enough to comprehend.
2. Moisten applicator with warm broth and insert into anus. Rotate to obtain specimen from rectal wall.
3. Place applicator in test tube and take to laboratory with completed SF 554 immediately.

S. DISCHARGES FROM WOUNDS OR CAVITIES
SMEAR

PURPOSE

To obtain a sample of wound discharges for laboratory examination.

EQUIPMENT

Sterile slides
Sterile applicators
Rubber bands - 2
Standard Form 554, Bacteriology

PROCEDURE

1. Tell patient what you are going to do.
2. Open package of slides, taking care not to contaminate them.
3. Take sample of discharge from wound using a sterile applicator.
4. Spread discharge lightly in center of slide.
5. Repeat for second slide. Discard applicators in paper bag for disposition in incinerator.
6. Place slides together so that specimens on each slide are in contact.
7. Put rubber bands around both slides, thus fastening them.
8. Take to laboratory immediately with request form.

POINTS TO EMPHASIZE

Indicate on SF 554 the examination desired.

COLLECTION OF SPECIMENS (Continued)

T. DISCHARGES FORM WOUNDS OR CAVITIES

CULTURE

PURPOSE

To collect specimen for laboratory analysis.

EQUIPMENT

Sterile culture tube containing a sterile cotton applicator, disposable
Standard Form 554, Bacteriology
For throat culture obtain special tube with special media from laboratory

PROCEDURE

1. Tell patient what you are going to do.
2. Remove cotton applicator from the tube; do not contaminate tip or stem of applicator.
3. Swab area to be cultured with applicator.
4. Replace applicator in tube and secure screw cap.
5. Take to laboratory immediately with completed SF 554.

PRECAUTION

Cultures must be taken to the laboratory immediately after being collected and handed to laboratory personnel. A dried out specimen is of no value.

IV. PREPARATION FOR RADIOLOGICAL STUDIES

A. ANGIOCARDIOGRAPHY

PURPOSE

To visualize by x-ray the heart and great blood vessels after a contrasting media is introduced through a vein.

EQUIPMENT

NPO sign
Preoperative medication as ordered
SF 522, Authorization Permit

PROCEDURE

1. Test dose of contrast media is given by Ward Medical Officer day prior to study.
2. Patient is given nothing by mouth after 2400 providing the examination is scheduled for the following morning.
3. Check patient's chart for signed permit (SF 522) and completed test results (CBC, urinalysis, chest x-ray).
4. Notify the x-ray department if patient has any known allergies.
5. Give preoperative medication as ordered.

AORTOGRAPHY AND ARTERIOGRAPHY

PURPOSE

To visualize by x-ray the aorta and arteries after a contrasting media has been injected.

EQUIPMENT

Same as for angiocardiography
Skin prep set for aortography

PROCEDURE

1. Skin preparation for aortography - prepare back from scapulae to sacrum.
2. Procedure is the same as for angiocardiography.
3. Give medication as ordered.

PREPARATION FOR RADIOLOGICAL STUDIES
B. ARTERIOGRAPHY (CEREBRAL)

PURPOSE

To visualize by x-ray the major vessels of the brain after a contrasting media has been injected, usually into the common carotid artery.

EQUIPMENT

NPO sign
Medication as ordered
Standard Form 519, Radiographic Report
Standard Form 522, Authorization Permit

PROCEDURE

1. Test dose of contrast media is given by Ward Medical Officer day prior to study.
2. Check with patient regarding allergies and notify the medical officer if allergies are reported.
3. Check patient's chart for signed permit SF 522.
4. Patient is given nothing by mouth after 2400.
5. Give preoperative medication as ordered one-half hour before sending patient to x-ray.
6. Completed SF 519A should accompany the patient.

PREPARATION FOR RADIOLOGICAL STUDIES
C. BRONCHOGRAM

PURPOSE

To visualize by x-ray the outlines of the bronchial tubes and their branches after a contrasting media is introduced through a cannula or an intratracheal catheter into the air passages.

EQUIPMENT

NPO sign
X-ray films
Standard Form 516, Operative Report
Standard Form 517, Anesthesia Report
Standard Form 522, Authorization Permit
Medication as ordered

PROCEDURE

1. Test dose of contrast media is given by Ward Medical Officer day prior to study.
2. Omit meal directly prior to examination:
   a. Nothing by mouth after 2400 if examination is to be done in the morning.
   b. Light liquid breakfast, no lunch if examination is scheduled to be done in the afternoon.
3. Include in patient's chart:
   a. One Operative Report, SF 516.
   b. Two Anesthesia Reports, SF 517 with carbon
   c. One Authorization Permit, 522. Signed.
4. Give medication as ordered.
5. Send patient to the x-ray department with his chart and x-ray films at appointed time.

PREPARATION FOR RADIOLOGICAL STUDIES

D. CHOLECYSTOGRAPHY

(Gallbladder Series)

PURPOSE

To prepare the patient for radiographic visualization of the common bile duct and gallbladder.

EQUIPMENT

NPO Sign
Radiopaque media

PROCEDURE

1. **Patient is given supper of dry toast, jelly, fruit and coffee or tea the evening preceding the examination.**
2. **Following the evening meal the patient is given six Telopaque tablets and instructed to take one every five minutes. (If other radiopaque media is used give as directed.)**
3. **Only water, clear tea or black coffee may be taken after ingestion of tablets.**
4. **Withhold breakfast on day of examination.**
5. **Send patient to x-ray department at scheduled time.**

PREPARATION FOR RADIOLOGICAL STUDIES
E. GASTROINTESTINAL SERIES

PURPOSE

To prepare the patient for diagnostic x-rays of the upper gastrointestinal tract.

EQUIPMENT

NPO sign

PROCEDURE

1. When examination is ordered, send Standard Form 519, Radiographic Report, to x-ray department for appointment.
2. Evening preceding the examination.
   a. Liquids may be taken after the evening meal until 2400. Nothing by mouth after 2400.
   b. Cathartic or enema is given before bedtime if ordered.
   c. No smoking or chewing gum after 2400.
3. On the day of the examination:
   a. Send patient to x-ray department at scheduled time - usually in the early morning.
   b. Noon meal and fluids are withheld until x-ray department confirms that no further x-rays are to be taken.
   c. Cathartic is given after noon meal is ordered.

PREPARATION OF RADIOLOGICAL STUDIES

F. BARIUM ENEMA

PURPOSE

To prepare the patient for a diagnostic x-ray of the lower gastro-intestinal tract.

EQUIPMENT

NPO sign

PROCEDURE

1. When examination is ordered, send Standard Form 519A, Radiographic Report, to the x-ray department for an appointment.
2. Day preceding the examination:
   a. Patient is to have nothing but low residue fluids after noon meal.
   b. Cathartic is given after noon meal if ordered.
   c. Cleansing enema is given at bedtime.
3. On the day of the examination:
   a. Enemas at 0600 until returns are clear.
   b. Send patient to x-ray department at scheduled time.
   c. When examination is completed a eathartic is given, if ordered.

PREPARATION OF RADIOLOGICAL STUDIES
G. INTRAVENOUS PYELOGRAM

PURPOSE

To visualize by x-ray the kidneys after a contrasting media has been injected intravenously.

EQUIPMENT

NPO sign
Standard Form SF 522, Authorization Permit

PROCEDURE

1. When examination is ordered, send Standard Form 519A, Radiographic Report, to the Urology Clinic for appointment.
2. Check patient's chart for signed permit, SF 522.
3. Test dose of contrast media is given by Ward Medical Officer day prior to study.
4. On evening preceding the examination:
   a. Give cathartic or other medication if ordered.
   b. Patient is instructed to take nothing by mouth after 2400.
5. On the morning of the examination, send patient to Urological x-ray department with chart at specified time.

RETROGRADE PYELOGRAM/CYSTOGRAPHY

PURPOSE

To visualize the bladder and ureters after a contrasting media has been introduced through the urethra.

PROCEDURE

1. Patient may have a light breakfast.
2. Force fluids prior to examination.
3. Send to Urological x-ray department with chart at specified time.
4. Standard Form 522, Authorization Permit, is required for this test.

PREPARATION FOR RADIOLOGICAL STUDIES
H. MYELOGRAM

PURPOSE

To visualize by x-ray the spinal canal after contrasting media is injected into the canal by means of a lumbar puncture.

EQUIPMENT

Skin prep set
Standard Form SF 522, Authorization Permit

PROCEDURE

1. When examination is ordered, send SF 519A, Radiographic Report, to the x-ray department for an appointment.
2. Test dose of contrast media is given by Ward Medical Officer day prior to study.
3. Check patient's chart for signed permit (SF 522).
4. If examination is to be done in the morning, the patient may have a light breakfast.
5. If examination is to be done in the afternoon, the patient may have a light lunch.
6. Shave lumbar area.
7. Give medication as ordered.
8. Send patient to x-ray on call with chart and previous x-rays.

PREPARATION FOR RADIOLOGICAL STUDIES
I. PNEUMOENCEPHALOGRAM

PURPOSE

To visualize by x-ray the cerebrospinal canal, and related structures of the brain and spinal cord.

EQUIPMENT

NPO sign
Standard Form SF 522, Authorization Permit

PROCEDURE

1. When examination is ordered, send SF 519A, Radiographic Report, to the x-ray department for an appointment.
2. Check patient's chart for signed permit (SF 522).
3. Patient is given nothing by mouth after 2400 the evening preceding the examination.
4. The day of the examination, give medication as ordered or when notified by x-ray department.
5. The procedure is usually done in the x-ray department.
6. Upon return of patient to the ward, carry out the medical officer's orders as to patient's activity.

V. BRONCHOSCOPY

PURPOSE

To directly view the respiratory tract.
To obtain tissue for biopsy.
To obtain pleural secretions for study.
To remove foreign bodies.

EQUIPMENT

NPO sign
X-ray films
Standard Form 522, Authorization Permit
Standard Form 515, Tissue Examination
Standard Form 516, Operative Report
Standard Form 517, Anesthesia Report
Two Standard Forms 554, Bacteriology
Medications as ordered

PROCEDURE

1. Omit meal directly prior to examination:
   a. Nothing by mouth after 2400 if examination is to be done in the morning.
   b. Liquids for breakfast and no lunch if examination is scheduled to be done in the afternoon.
2. Include in patient's chart:
   a. One Tissue Examination Sheet, SF 515.
   b. Two Anesthesia Reports, SF 517 with carbon.
   c. One Operative Report, SF 516.
   d. Two Bacteriology Reports, SF 554.
   e. Signed Authorization Permit, SF 522.
3. Give medication as ordered.
4. Send patient with his chart and x-ray films to operating room or bronchoscopy department when called or ordered.

POINTS TO EMPHASIZE

1. Nothing by mouth after examination until all sensation has returned to patient's throat.
2. No smoking until sensation returns to patient's throat.

VI. T-3, T-4 TEST

PURPOSE

To determine the level of thyroid hormone, thyroxin, in the patient's circulating blood stream.

EQUIPMENT

NPO sign
Sterile syringe, 10 cc.
Sterile needle - 20-21 gauge, 1 1/4" length
Blood tube, red top
Standard Form 549, Hematology

PROCEDURE

1. Nothing by mouth after 2400.
2. On the morning of the test, send patient to laboratory if ambulatory or execute venipuncture on ward.
3. Draw 10 cc. blood and place in red top blood tube.
4. Send tube and Standard Form 549 to laboratory immediately.
5. Patient may have breakfast following venipuncture.

POINTS TO EMPHASIZE

1. Clotted blood is necessary for this test.

CARE OF EQUIPMENT

1. Break off tip of needle and syringe. Dispose of syringe and needle according to local instruction.

VII. COLD PRESSOR TEST

PURPOSE

To determine vascular hyperactivity.

EQUIPMENT

Sphygmomanometer and stethoscope
Basin ice water
Pen
Standard Form 512, Plotting Chart

PROCEDURE

1. Have patient remain in supine position for 20 - 60 minutes before and throughout test.
2. Place blood pressure cuff on arm.
3. Several readings of the blood pressure are taken during this time, until a basal level has been established.
4. Immerse hand and wrist of opposite arm in ice water 4° C. for 60 seconds and check the blood pressure at 30 and 60 second intervals during immersion.
5. Take blood pressure every two minutes thereafter until basal level is again reached.
6. Graph blood pressure reading before, during and after immersion, on SF-512.

VIII. ABDOMINAL PARACENTESIS

PURPOSE

To aspirate fluid from the abdominal cavity.

EQUIPMENT

Sterile paracentesis tray
Sterile gloves
Sterile specimen container
Local anesthesia solution
Alcohol sponges
Skin disinfectant solution
Protective sheet or pads
Large basin for abdominal fluid
Dry sterile dressing
Adhesive tape
Abdominal or scultetus binder
Standard Form 557, Miscellaneous
Standard Form 522, Authorization Permit

PROCEDURE

1. Check chart for signed permit (SF 522).
2. Wash hands.
3. Assemble equipment. Take to bedside.
4. Screen patient and tell him what you are going to do.
5. Have patient empty bladder.
6. Position patient:
   a. Sitting position on side of bed with back and feet supported.
   b. Reclining position - semi-Fowler position in bed.
7. Place protective sheet or pads in position.
8. Place large basin on covered foot stool at bedside.
9. Assist medical officer:
   a. Open sterile tray.
   b. Pour solution for skin preparation.
   c. Cleanse top of local anesthesia solution bottle with alcohol sponge. Hold while medical officer draws solution into syringe.
10. Support the patient physically and mentally during the procedure.
11. Apply dry sterile dressings and binder after treatment is completed. Montgomery straps are used if frequent dressing changes are anticipated. Leave patient comfortable.
12. Measure amount of fluid obtained. Send labeled specimen to laboratory with Standard Form 557.
13. Chart description and amount of fluid and effect of treatment on patient on Nursing Notes and Intake and Output sheet, if applicable.

POINTS TO EMPHASIZE

1. Shave abdomen if necessary.
2. Watch patient for signs of shock as evidenced by color change, pulse, respiration and profuse perspiration.
3. Provide protection for mattress if patient's incision is to be draining.
4. If procedure is done in the treatment room, always assist patient back to bed.

CARE OF EQUIPMENT

1. Wash equipment with warm soapy water. Rinse and return to CSR.
2. Discard disposable items.

IX. LUMBAR PUNCTURE

PURPOSE

To aspirate cerebrospinal fluid.

EQUIPMENT

Sterile Lumbar Puncture Tray
Sterile spinal manometer
Sterile gloves
Skin disinfectant solution
Local anesthesia solution
Protective sheet or pads
Curved basin
Stool or chair
Three Standard Forms 555, Spinal Fluid, and one 554, Microbiology
Standard Form 522, Authorization Permit

PROCEDURE

1. Check patient's chart for signed permit (SF 522).
2. Wash hands.
3. Assemble equipment. Take to bedside.
4. Screen patient and tell him what you are going to do.
5. Place protective sheet or pads in position.
6. Assist medical officer:
   a. Open sterile tray.
   b. Pour solution for skin preparation.
   c. Pour local anesthesia solution into a sterile medicine glass or hold bottle for medical officer to aspirate desired amount.
7. Position patient:
   a. Place patient on his side with back near the edge of the bed.
   b. Flex the body by bringing the knees as close to the chin as possible.
8. Standing on opposite side of bed from medical officer, help patient to maintain correct position by placing one hand on patient's head and second hand under patient's knees.
9. Reassure and support patient mentally during procedure.
10. Apply dressing to site of injection after treatment is completed.
11. Make patient comfortable.
12. Label specimens and send immediately to the laboratory with proper forms.
13. Chart description and approximate amount of fluid, number of specimens sent to the laboratory and effect of treatment on patient on Nursing Notes (SF 510).

LUMBAR PUNCTURE (Continued)

POINTS TO EMPHASIZE

1. Send the specimen to the laboratory immediately and deliver directly to laboratory personnel, since examination should be done within 30 minutes after specimen is obtained.
2. Instruct the patient to remain flat in bed, as ordered after treatment.
3. Three SF 555 are required for routine examination.
   Label: one for chemistry
   one for serology
   one for cell count

X. THORACENTESIS

PURPOSE

To aspirate fluid from the chest.

EQUIPMENT

Sterile Thoracentesis Tray
Sterile gloves
Sterile graduated container
Local anesthesia solution
Dry sterile dressings
Alcohol sponges
Skin disinfectant solution
Pillow with plastic pillowcase
Protective sheet or pads
Adhesive tape
Standard Form 557, Miscellaneous, and 554, Microbiology
Standard Form 522, Authorization Permit

PROCEDURE

1. Check chart for signed permit (SF 522).
2. Wash hands.
3. Assemble equipment. Take to bedside.
4. Screen patient and tell him what you are going to do.
5. Place protective sheet or pads in position.
6. Assist medical officer:
   a. Open sterile tray.
   b. Pour solution for skin preparation.
   c. Cleanse top of local anesthesia bottle with alcohol sponge. Hold while medical officer draws solution into syringe.
7. Position patient:
   a. Sitting position - on side of bed with feet resting on chair. Place overbed table with pillow on it in front of patient. Instruct him to rest his head and fold arms on pillow.
   b. Reclining position - on unaffected side close to edge of bed.
8. Reassure and support the patient physically and mentally during procedure.
9. Apply dry sterile dressings over wound after treatment is completed. Leave patient comfortable.
10. Measure amount of fluid obtained. Label specimen and send to laboratory with SF 557.
11. Chart description and amount of fluid and effect on patient on Nursing Notes (SF 510) and Intake and Output chart, if applicable.

POINTS TO EMPHASIZE

1. Watch patient for signs of shock as evidenced by changes in color, pulse, respiration and profuse perspiration.
2. If the procedure is done in the treatment room, always assist patient back to bed.

CARE OF EQUIPMENT

1. Wash equipment with warm soapy water. Rinse and return to CSR.
2. Discard disposable items.

ANSWER SHEET

TEST NO. ______________ PART ______ TITLE OF POSITION ______________________________
(AS GIVEN IN EXAMINATION ANNOUNCEMENT - INCLUDE OPTION, IF ANY)

PLACE OF EXAMINATION ______________________ (CITY OR TOWN) ______________ (STATE) DATE ______

RATING

USE THE SPECIAL PENCIL. MAKE GLOSSY BLACK MARKS.

1	A B C D E	26	A B C D E	51	A B C D E	76	A B C D E	101	A B C D E
2	A B C D E	27	A B C D E	52	A B C D E	77	A B C D E	102	A B C D E
3	A B C D E	28	A B C D E	53	A B C D E	78	A B C D E	103	A B C D E
4	A B C D E	29	A B C D E	54	A B C D E	79	A B C D E	104	A B C D E
5	A B C D E	30	A B C D E	55	A B C D E	80	A B C D E	105	A B C D E
6	A B C D E	31	A B C D E	56	A B C D E	81	A B C D E	106	A B C D E
7	A B C D E	32	A B C D E	57	A B C D E	82	A B C D E	107	A B C D E
8	A B C D E	33	A B C D E	58	A B C D E	83	A B C D E	108	A B C D E
9	A B C D E	34	A B C D E	59	A B C D E	84	A B C D E	109	A B C D E
10	A B C D E	35	A B C D E	60	A B C D E	85	A B C D E	110	A B C D E

Make only ONE mark for each answer. Additional and stray marks may be counted as mistakes. In making corrections, erase errors COMPLETELY.

11	A B C D E	36	A B C D E	61	A B C D E	86	A B C D E	111	A B C D E
12	A B C D E	37	A B C D E	62	A B C D E	87	A B C D E	112	A B C D E
13	A B C D E	38	A B C D E	63	A B C D E	88	A B C D E	113	A B C D E
14	A B C D E	39	A B C D E	64	A B C D E	89	A B C D E	114	A B C D E
15	A B C D E	40	A B C D E	65	A B C D E	90	A B C D E	115	A B C D E
16	A B C D E	41	A B C D E	66	A B C D E	91	A B C D E	116	A B C D E
17	A B C D E	42	A B C D E	67	A B C D E	92	A B C D E	117	A B C D E
18	A B C D E	43	A B C D E	68	A B C D E	93	A B C D E	118	A B C D E
19	A B C D E	44	A B C D E	69	A B C D E	94	A B C D E	119	A B C D E
20	A B C D E	45	A B C D E	70	A B C D E	95	A B C D E	120	A B C D E
21	A B C D E	46	A B C D E	71	A B C D E	96	A B C D E	121	A B C D E
22	A B C D E	47	A B C D E	72	A B C D E	97	A B C D E	122	A B C D E
23	A B C D E	48	A B C D E	73	A B C D E	98	A B C D E	123	A B C D E
24	A B C D E	49	A B C D E	74	A B C D E	99	A B C D E	124	A B C D E
25	A B C D E	50	A B C D E	75	A B C D E	100	A B C D E	125	A B C D E

ANSWER SHEET

TEST NO. ______________ PART ________ TITLE OF POSITION ______________________________
(AS GIVEN IN EXAMINATION ANNOUNCEMENT - INCLUDE OPTION, IF ANY)

PLACE OF EXAMINATION ______________________________ (CITY OR TOWN) ______________ (STATE) DATE ______________

RATING

USE THE SPECIAL PENCIL. MAKE GLOSSY BLACK MARKS.

1 A B C D E	26 A B C D E	51 A B C D E	76 A B C D E	101 A B C D E
2 A B C D E	27 A B C D E	52 A B C D E	77 A B C D E	102 A B C D E
3 A B C D E	28 A B C D E	53 A B C D E	78 A B C D E	103 A B C D E
4 A B C D E	29 A B C D E	54 A B C D E	79 A B C D E	104 A B C D E
5 A B C D E	30 A B C D E	55 A B C D E	80 A B C D E	105 A B C D E
6 A B C D E	31 A B C D E	56 A B C D E	81 A B C D E	106 A B C D E
7 A B C D E	32 A B C D E	57 A B C D E	82 A B C D E	107 A B C D E
8 A B C D E	33 A B C D E	58 A B C D E	83 A B C D E	108 A B C D E
9 A B C D E	34 A B C D E	59 A B C D E	84 A B C D E	109 A B C D E
10 A B C D E	35 A B C D E	60 A B C D E	85 A B C D E	110 A B C D E

Make only ONE mark for each answer. Additional and stray marks may be counted as mistakes. In making corrections, erase errors COMPLETELY.

11 A B C D E	36 A B C D E	61 A B C D E	86 A B C D E	111 A B C D E
12 A B C D E	37 A B C D E	62 A B C D E	87 A B C D E	112 A B C D E
13 A B C D E	38 A B C D E	63 A B C D E	88 A B C D E	113 A B C D E
14 A B C D E	39 A B C D E	64 A B C D E	89 A B C D E	114 A B C D E
15 A B C D E	40 A B C D E	65 A B C D E	90 A B C D E	115 A B C D E
16 A B C D E	41 A B C D E	66 A B C D E	91 A B C D E	116 A B C D E
17 A B C D E	42 A B C D E	67 A B C D E	92 A B C D E	117 A B C D E
18 A B C D E	43 A B C D E	68 A B C D E	93 A B C D E	118 A B C D E
19 A B C D E	44 A B C D E	69 A B C D E	94 A B C D E	119 A B C D E
20 A B C D E	45 A B C D E	70 A B C D E	95 A B C D E	120 A B C D E
21 A B C D E	46 A B C D E	71 A B C D E	96 A B C D E	121 A B C D E
22 A B C D E	47 A B C D E	72 A B C D E	97 A B C D E	122 A B C D E
23 A B C D E	48 A B C D E	73 A B C D E	98 A B C D E	123 A B C D E
24 A B C D E	49 A B C D E	74 A B C D E	99 A B C D E	124 A B C D E
25 A B C D E	50 A B C D E	75 A B C D E	100 A B C D E	125 A B C D E